C000113501

Outback Teacher

Outback Teacher

The inspiring story of a remarkable young woman,
life with her students and their
adventures in remote Australia

Sally Gare
with Freda Marnie

ALLEN&UNWIN
SYDNEY • MELBOURNE • AUCKLAND • LONDON

All photographs are from Sally Gare's personal collection.

First published in 2022

Copyright © Sally Gare and Freda Marnie 2022

All rights reserved. No part of this book may be reproduced or transmitted in any form or by any means, electronic or mechanical, including photocopying, recording or by any information storage and retrieval system, without prior permission in writing from the publisher. The Australian *Copyright Act 1968* (the Act) allows a maximum of one chapter or 10 per cent of this book, whichever is the greater, to be photocopied by any educational institution for its educational purposes provided that the educational institution (or body that administers it) has given a remuneration notice to the Copyright Agency (Australia) under the Act.

Allen & Unwin
83 Alexander Street
Crows Nest NSW 2065
Australia
Phone: (61 2) 8425 0100
Email: info@allenandunwin.com
Web: www.allenandunwin.com

A catalogue record for this
book is available from the
National Library of Australia

ISBN 978 1 76106 534 7

Maps by Mika Tabata
Set in 12/18pt Sabon by Midland Typesetters, Australia
Printed and bound in Australia by McPherson's Printing Group

10 9 8 7 6 5 4 3 2 1

The paper in this book is FSC® certified. FSC® promotes environmentally responsible, socially beneficial and economically viable management of the world's forests.

Aboriginal and Torres Strait Islander people are advised that this work contains the names and images of individuals who may have passed away and that some historical language has been used.

We acknowledge the traditional owners of Country throughout Australia and their connections to land, sea and community. We pay our respects to their Elders past and present and extend that respect to all Aboriginal and Torres Strait Islander peoples.

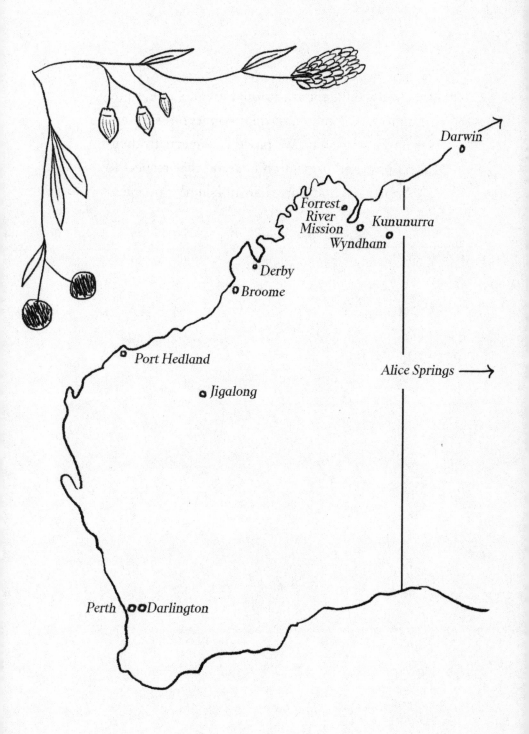

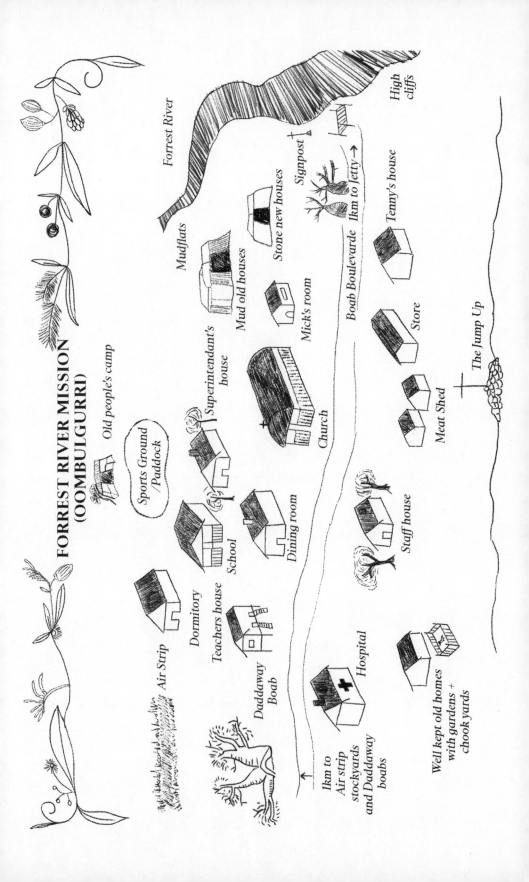

FORREST RIVER MISSION (OOMBULGURRI)

Forrest River

Old people's camp

Mudflats

Superintendant's house

Mud old houses

Stone new houses

Mick's room

Signpost

1km to Jetty →

Boab Boulevarde

Tenny's house

Sports Ground / Paddock

Church

Store

Air Strip

Dormitory

School

Teachers house

Dining room

Staff house

Meat Shed

Daddaway Boab

High cliffs

The Jump Up

Hospital

1km to
Air strip
stockyards
and Daddaway
boabs

Well kept old homes
with gardens +
chook yards

PORT HEDLAND AS I REMEMBER IT IN 1961

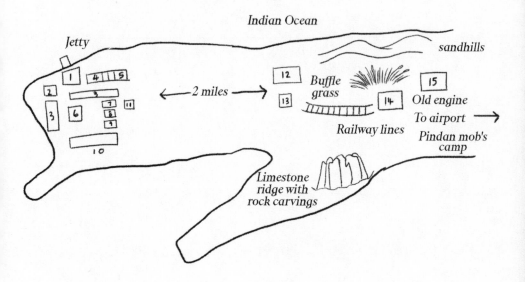

Indian Ocean

Jetty

sandhills

2 miles

Buffle grass

Old engine

To airport

Railway lines

Pindan mob's camp

Limestone ridge with rock carvings

1 Tennis and Basketball Courts
2 Pier Hotel
3 Shops & Offices
4 Esplanade Hotel
5 Elders Shop
6 Open Air Picture Gardens
7 Catholic School
8 Glasses' Home
9 Anglican Church
10 Offices & Homes
11 United Church
12 New School on the Hill
13 Nun's House
14 Loco School
15 Native Hospital

1

HEADING NORTH

With the threat of a cyclone imminent, we were having a cloudy, wet and bumpy trip in the Douglas DC-3. It was February 1956 and I was just out of teachers' college, heading to my first posting, an Aboriginal mission run by the Church of England. Forrest River Mission, or FRM as it was sometimes known, was outside Wyndham, near the Western Australian and Northern Territory border.

The trip by plane to Wyndham from Perth was a 3200-kilometre journey up the west coast of the vast state of Western Australia. With stops at Geraldton, Carnarvon, Port Hedland, Broome, Derby and finally Wyndham, the flight could take up to thirteen hours, depending on loading and unloading of people and supplies at each airport. The DC-3 we were flying up in was an unpressurised twin-propeller plane that could carry up to twenty-eight passengers, and we were bounced around through the hot, rough air of the tropical north for literally hours on end. Two of my travelling companions on that first trip north were the mission's new matron, Mrs O'Reilly, and her young son Mick. We hadn't talked much on the way up as the poor matron was unwell from the turbulent weather.

People used to say if you lived in Wyndham you didn't go to hell when you died; you'd already been there. It was hot and, in February, extremely humid, a far cry from Perth's dry heat. After we arrived, the unsteady matron, her son and I caught the airline bus from the airport to town. I was quite concerned about her; she didn't look well.

In my first glimpse of the nor'west town, as we headed down the main street leading to the port, I was amazed at the strange bulbous bottle-shaped trunks of the large boab trees that were dotted along the street. Nearly all the buildings in the main street—a two-storey pub, one cafe and a few shops—were made out of corrugated iron.

I later learnt that the twenty-bed hospital had only one permanent doctor, and that any serious cases had to be flown to Derby with the Royal Flying Doctor Service (RFDS). The meat works was the biggest employer, but it only operated between July and September, the coolest time to be there.

The population of Wyndham at this time numbered about four hundred white people living in town and two hundred Aboriginal people living out in two camps, Three Mile and Six Mile, named for their distance from the centre of town. We called people black and white back then and, even with the work I do today, my Aboriginal friends don't mind me saying black or white to describe ourselves.

The mission's handyman, Bob Morrow, met us in town. He too was concerned about the matron's health and tried to get us accommodation in town at the pub for the night so she could rest up. When he found there wasn't a spare room, he decided we'd go out on the late afternoon tide. I had no idea what that would entail but was about to find out.

There was a huge difference in the water levels between high and low tide at Wyndham. That day in early February, the incoming tide would be at 9 p.m. and 3 a.m., and we aimed to be at the mouth of the Forrest River for the 9 p.m. change to make it all the way up the river to the mission. When the tide was on its way out in Wyndham, as it was on this occasion, we were forced to walk out for about fifty metres over wet rocks and broken glass.

With Bob leading the way, we waded out to the little open four-metre launch, holding our luggage over our heads. When we finally clambered in over its side, we found it was already full, occupied by the local Oombulgurri people and mission supplies. So, we squeezed in where we could just as night fell. It was only when we were on the boat that I learnt we had been lucky not to see any saltwater crocodiles!

The dirt road to Oombulgurri from Wyndham was yet to be fully constructed. It would ultimately be about 210 kilometres long, but it was pretty much a rough, uncharted track back then, prone to washouts from the summer Wet Season. To get safely to the mission, you basically needed to go by either boat or plane.

It felt like quite an adventure as we putted out into the West Arm of the Cambridge Gulf and then waited at the mouth of the Forrest River for the tide to change from outgoing to incoming, to take us all the way to the upper reaches of the river, and on to the mission. Despite having left Perth at five that morning, and with night upon us, we still had a long way to go. Bob told us that it could take anything from eight hours to thirteen hours to travel the sixty miles (one hundred kilometres) from Wyndham to the mission along the windy Forrest River, more if you became stuck in the mud. In the time ahead, I was to find that this happened quite often.

Bob expertly brewed us a cup of tea to while away the time as we waited for the tide to change. When young Mick O'Reilly complained to his mother that he was hungry, I heard her tell him, 'You're in the bush now. What you can't do today, there's always tomorrow—that includes eating.' I nodded silently to myself in agreement. I was expecting a very basic, isolated time ahead, but I was determined to do it.

As kids we had raised funds for missions. I remember being praised at Sunday School for a rhyme that I made up; I can still remember it—'To help the Natives we need nurses/ So please be kind and open your purses'. As a child I had seen people who worked on missions, helping our Indigenous peoples, supplying food, healthcare and teaching; now that I had graduated, I was keen to go out and help.

As we made our way into the Forrest River, instead of thinking of the hardships that might lie ahead, I gazed out into the darkness, trying to differentiate the distant riverbank from the dark water, seeing the reflection of the lights of our little launch in the eyes of one crocodile as we passed.

It was still night when we finally reached the mission. Thick cloud obliterated any hope of moonlight, but we were met by a whole host of welcoming people, including most of my soon-to-be students who, despite the hour, were keen to see their new teacher. My first sight of the mission was via patchy torchlight as I walked through the tall cane grass.

Eventually I was shown my new home, a little two-room flat on stilts with modern fibro walls and roof. Inside my flat was a sitting room with a single chair and desk and another room to the side containing my single bed. I quickly fell sleep, eager to see what the mission looked like in daylight.

2

DJIDJA

I woke the next morning in a lather of sweat. The mission had a small generator that was turned on for lights at night, but only for about two or three hours, depending on the time of year, as the fuel to run the generators was expensive and had to be brought in with all the other supplies on the little mission launch. There was no power at all during the day, and certainly no fans or air conditioning.

Going out into the day I was greeted by some of my students, and I thought them the most adorable crowd I had ever met. They all seemed to love cuddles and treated me with more respect than many white kids I'd been around. I joined a game they were playing, similar to rounders with a bat and ball, though without a score. If the ball was caught, you were out, and there were no arguments. They all seemed gentle with each other, although the game was fast paced and caused many shrieks, especially when their new teacher had a go, took an almighty swing and missed!

I was greeted by the mission superintendent, Bill Jamison, and his wife. Mary Jamison was very quiet and calm, and told me that she found this to be her method for being on a mission. Mary had been at Forrest River for ten years, arriving and working as a teacher. Her future husband Bill arrived four years after she had, and they had married at the mission not long after. Their marriage had been officiated by the mission chaplain, Father Coaldrake, whom I would later meet, and they had their honeymoon camping at one of the creeks near the mission.

Bill and Mary gave me a tour of my new home. We chatted as we walked back down to the river. Bill would have probably been in his thirties then. Bill and Mary had three little boys, I think, and they asked me about my family back in faraway Perth. I ran through my family, including my uncle, the Rev. Ralph Thomas who Bill knew as Ralph and was on the Perth committee that oversaw the mission. He had been thrilled that I was going to Forrest River, and his wife, Aunty Coral, had made me a farewell cake with an open-mouthed crocodile on top.

The school was behind the teacher's fibro 'house' that sat high on stilts. This was where the other teacher, who was yet to arrive, and I had a small unit each. The school was started and had been run by the Church, but became a government school just three years earlier. It was more like a shelter than a classroom, which did take me a bit by surprise. I couldn't imagine a class full of white kids being educated in it. It had a large, corrugated iron roof held up by tall poles, with walls made out of dry cane grass stuffed between chicken wire and a rammed ant-bed floor. The walls weren't even a metre high. The space above the wall acted like an open breezeway, letting any passing puff of wind go through to cool anyone inside.

I had met up with the other teacher, Lisa (not her real name), in Perth in the Christmas holidays. She was quite a bit older than me and was well qualified. It was unusual back then for a female teacher to be the head of a school, but the government seemed perfectly happy to let Lisa run this school. She made it obvious to me that she was pretty upset that a newly qualified teacher was being sent up. She'd already been teaching at the school a year, and I was replacing another, more experienced teacher who had been there for three years.

Lisa caught the steamboat up the coast from Perth, having left not long after we first met. It could take up to three weeks to make it to the mission, but she had assured me she would be there at the start of the school year. I took the plane up because my dad was the general manager for MacRobertson Miller Airlines (MMA), which flew passengers and freight all over the North West, and I was eligible for discounted travel and freight, something that would help in countless ways in the future. Bill was concerned that Lisa might be held up by a cyclone that was heading towards Derby, but he said we could only wait and see.

Behind the school was a dormitory built for about twenty kids, who were looked after by an Oombulgurri couple, Robert and Louisa Roberts, who themselves had been born and raised at the mission. All the white staff were called Brother so-and-so or Sister so-and-so because, as Louisa pointed out, we're all brothers (*abela* in Oombulgurri) and sisters (*djidja*) in God's sight. I became Djidja Gare. My first Oombulgurri word.

The dormitory, made of stone and concrete, was always locked at night. Boys were usually kept at the dormitory until they were ten and would then be moved out into one of the family groups at the mission; the girls stayed until they finished school. The youngest were Angus and Ann, aged three and four, and the eldest was Una, who was thought to be sixteen. If the birthdate of the dormitory kids was not known when they arrived, they were given 1 July—there were seven kids who shared that same birthdate.

Two of the older dormitory girls, Connie Smith and Judy Taylor, had to be sent to Wyndham for leprosy tests not long after I arrived. When I first met Judy, she kept hiding her hands. Connie would go on to write a very philosophical letter back to the mission explaining she knew she was in God's care and that she wasn't surprised she had to be tested, as her mother had leprosy. The girls were very homesick and frightened about sleeping anywhere other than in a locked dormitory. Connie came back, as she didn't have leprosy, but Judy was diagnosed with it. I'm unsure what happened to her, but she was probably sent to a leprosarium, as was common then for anyone, Aboriginal or non-Aboriginal, diagnosed with the disease.

Over half of the dormitory kids had white or Afghan heritage, as well as Aboriginal heritage. I presumed the dormitory kids were orphans but was later told that the station owners sent them in for an education. It was rare for Aboriginal people to receive an education in the fifties, and it was only years later that I realised they were probably part of the 'Stolen Generation'. At twenty years of age, I didn't know that term, nor understand its horrid implications.

Behind the dormitory sat the sportsground, and behind that, outside the mission compound, was the 'old people's camp'. Eight families lived there in a collection of bush humpies. The older people lived a more traditional cultural life. Not wanting to give up their many wives and dogs, they didn't attend the white man's church and the camp was where traditional corroborees were held every Friday. Everyone—Aboriginal and non-Aboriginal—was welcome to attend, but occasionally the men held a secret one to which no women were allowed.

There were about thirty-five older people living at the camp, and over forty dogs. There were dogs everywhere, so many of them that the Wyndham police would come through every now and then and cull them so they didn't become a nuisance around the mission. The old people would come into the mission and get rations or go to the hospital for whatever medical help they needed, then they would head back out to their camp. The younger family groups stayed within the compound.

The main mission buildings were set on either side of an avenue of boab trees that had been planted by the early missionaries forty years earlier, though they didn't yet have the huge bulbous trunks that I had seen in Wyndham. Bill explained that there was a cluster of large boabs past the mission; it was a regular meeting place and was known as Daddaway. 'Ask anyone at the mission where it is,' he explained, 'and they'll point you in its direction, with their chins, and tell you, "Daddaway!"' This was also the direction of the airstrip and stockyards for working cattle.

Heading towards the river, the next building down the avenue from the teacher's house was the staff dining room. All staff meals were cooked by the matron and served in the communal dining room, and we could wash ourselves and our clothes in the nearby staff ablution block, with other blocks dotted around the mission for all to use.

The hospital and staff quarters sat across the avenue. The hospital was a solid structure made of stone and concrete, with solid shutter-type windows consisting of a wooden slab that could be propped open or pulled shut depending on the weather. The next building along was the chaplain's house and a cottage being built for Connie MacDonald, an Aboriginal kindergarten teacher from Alice Springs whom I was yet to meet.

Next to the hospital were the staff quarters and across the avenue was Mission House occupied by Bill, Mary and their young family. Mission House was also home to the pedal radio, our only way of communicating with the outside world.

The Church of St Michael, where Bill and Mary had been married, was the largest building at the mission. It was built in a similar style to the school with a large, corrugated iron roof, head-high walls, about 6 feet with a gap to let a breeze through, and it had a hard-packed ant-bed floor with an altar at the end. Next door to this sat Father's house, another building built in the same style as the hospital.

The building closest to the river was Tennyson Thompson's house and the mission store. 'Tenny' was then in his seventies, a Gallipoli veteran who had worked at the mission for the previous twenty-eight or so years; he tended to keep very much to himself. He was in charge of the store and was the chief 'bell' ringer—the bell being a big metal bar hanging from a large boab tree outside the church, which he struck with an old crankshaft at six every morning to start the day. All of the Oombulgurri adults worked in return for rations.

The men worked with Bill and the white handymen; the women worked in the hospital, the kitchen and the student dormitory, or they cleaned the staff houses. Rations and supplies were handed out from Tenny's corrugated iron store next door once a week, or whenever the launch brought in supplies.

There were thirty Oombulgurri families living at the mission, twenty-four of them in the compound, with their houses opposite Tenny's store. Their houses were mostly one-roomed and were made of ant bed and mud, some with fences and yards that were swept every morning. For the white staff, most of their cottages were weatherboard, where the termites also loved to make their homes.

The compound gates opened from the avenue onto the river and jetty, where the launch was tied up. I'm glad I hadn't seen how rickety the mission jetty was when we'd arrived in the dark and walked the few hundred metres up through the towering cane grass into the mission compound.

A community hall was still being built when I arrived. There was also an administration building, workshops, the powerhouse, several long-drop toilets, plus shower rooms with laundries attached for all to use. The toilet was often a place where you'd encounter some of the local wildlife. It was a rough wooden structure (made from old packing cases) over a very deep hole. After I sat down very carefully to avoid splinters, I would often have to rise quickly as something else decided to crawl around below—sometimes you had to remove up to three frogs and a lizard before using it. The frogs also particularly liked my room and made a noise like someone scraping their fingers over a balloon, all a bit off-putting at first.

The animal life around the mission was incredible, including giant frogs, snakes and crocodiles, both freshwater and saltwater. The latter were the ones to really fear: you might get a nip from a freshie, but the saltwater crocs were the man-eaters.

Everywhere the trees, grasses and flowers, like the animals, all tended to be enormous. The Forrest River, as it ran back downstream to the gulf, was bordered by steep red cliffs and saltwater croc–infested islands, before coming out into mud flats where the launch at low tide would often get stuck. Upstream from the mission the Forrest River changed into a freshwater river before petering out into beautiful lily-covered billabongs that held the not-as-nasty freshwater crocs. In the distance were great, red-stoned gorges.

On my first afternoon there, I walked to a nearby fresh waterfall with some of the dormitory girls. They went for a *bogi* (swim) and then sat on the flat-topped shelves over which the water fell. They laughed, screamed and splashed. As we walked to and from the mission, the cane grass was well above our heads. The river and waterways were teeming with great flocks of ducks, magpie geese, pelicans, brolgas and white cockatoos; with huge barramundi and other fish; with giant green frogs, turtles and various goannas, lizards and snakes.

At the beginning of 1956, there would be fifteen whites living at Forrest River Mission. A few white staff assisted Bill Jamison to run the mission, overseen by a committee of the Perth Diocese. Bill and his wife, Mary, and their three boys were joined by Father Coaldrake and his wife and their son; plus Harold Weibye (the mission's stockman and an ex-alcoholic); Tennyson 'Tenny' Thompson; Mrs O'Reilly and her son, Mick; Bob Morrow, the handyman and launch operator; myself; and Lisa, when she arrived. With eight white mission staff to meet the needs of over 160 Aboriginal people, it wouldn't take long to realise that we were horribly under-staffed. Unlike the talkative Oombulgurri, the white staff did not ask questions, nor did they speak unnecessarily, so I initially didn't find out much about any of the staff. I didn't mind. As an eager young teacher straight out of college, my focus was on my school kids and teaching.

3

IN THE BACKGROUND

When I went to teachers' college in the fifties, there was a scholarship system in place. During the two years that I studied to be a teacher, the government paid my fees and provided me with a living allowance. This was on the proviso that I spent my first two years of teaching somewhere in the country, accepting a lower rate of pay, before taking a city or suburban posting. I had put Carnarvon down as my first choice for a placement as I'd visited the area a couple of times as a child; my older brother John and I had stayed on a sheep station with friends. I'd also heard Dad talk with concern about the lack of education for Aboriginal kids in the Pilbara area. In 1956 there wasn't a vacancy anywhere in the Pilbara or Carnarvon, but there was one at Forrest River.

The mission was a place with much history, both Aboriginal and non-Aboriginal, both good and bad. It was started by the Church of England in 1896 but was abandoned after the son of the then bishop of Perth was speared and clubbed a few months after starting the mission. It was restarted in

1913 by a more experienced missionary, the Reverend Ernest Gribble.

Trouble came in 1926, when a white man, Fred Hay, was killed near the mission by a spear thrown by an Aboriginal man by the name of Lumbra. Various stories came out later in the press; some said there was a dispute over a woman, others said the murder was an act of self-defence. The locals told me that it was because Hay had found some spears beside a waterfall and broken them so they couldn't be used. Lumbra saw him doing this and attacked him, then ran away.

When a search party was sent out from Wyndham in search of Lumbra, a massacre resulted, with many Aboriginal people being shot and their bodies burnt. Lumbra and two witnesses were eventually sent to Wyndham, where he was tried and apparently sentenced to death. My Forrest River friends blamed Lumbra for running away, which had caused the death of so many innocents.

The massacre site was about thirty-five kilometres from the mission; many Oombulgurri would not go out there because of bad spirits. Some said they could hear the sound of a mother crying over her dead baby when they went there, so most avoided the area.

There was a memorial to the 1926 massacre at the mission. It was a simple cross made out of galvanised pipe and sat on the high ridge known as the Jump Up, which was at the back of the mission. Each day the sun would set behind that cross. It was only thirty years on from that horrible event when I arrived.

It rained, drizzled and thundered for seemingly days on end—part of the cyclone that would isolate Derby and hold up the arrival of Lisa. Everything was damp and even the sandals I was wearing began to swell as they absorbed the surrounding moisture. The humidity was stifling, and a thick cloud of insects seemed to be everywhere. I was bitten by sandflies and was also suffering from prickly heat; not a good start, I thought.

Each morning would start with Tenny hitting the rising bell. Church was at 6.15, though for my first service it was just myself, Father Coaldrake, Robert and Louisa Roberts and the dormitory kids. It was certainly different from what I was used to. We'd been brought up initially as Church of England (later known as Anglican) and then became Quakers or 'Friends', following Dad's change of religion after the Second World War. I was the second of five children, with one older brother, John, then Bob after me, then Anne and a bit of a gap until the baby of the family, Susie, arrived a few months before the end of the Second World War. We had a loving family, in which religion played an important part. Everyone seemed to go to church or follow a religion more diligently back then.

A Friends meeting would always start with an hour of meditation. People only spoke during the meeting if they felt strongly led to do so. I remember the first time I spoke in a meeting in Darlington. I was probably about fifteen and remember realising why the Society of Friends were known as the Quakers. I was feeling pretty nervous, and was quaking, but felt that I had something worthwhile to say. I broke the silence and said something like, 'We hear that the ideal Christian way of life is "following the straight and narrow"— go to church, be honest, don't drink and gamble, stay away from bad people, be prim and proper. Wouldn't it be better to think of all the good things we can do? Perhaps take a windy path with lots of little tracks going off it. Be with the lonely, help the missions, work with the United Nations, make friends with unpopular people and look for as many different ways as possible to make God's world a better place?' I remember the lovely feeling when Dad thanked me after the meeting for my contribution.

I enjoyed my first service at the mission; it was certainly different from a Friends meeting, but I felt I was still communing with God. After church each day, Bill Jamison and Harold would allocate work—fencing, collecting wood, building, maintenance and stock work, gardening in the vegetable plot, or butchering a bullock or a goat, which had to be shot and then brought in with the tractor and trailer. The Oombulgurri men worked hard, and often without supervision.

There were still a few days until school started so I helped Matron in the hospital because the mission nurse hadn't yet arrived. Matron was usually assisted by two or three Oombul-gurri women who were learning basic nursing. I was shown how to give an injection, the first person I injected ending up being myself—a shot of antibiotics for an infected insect bite.

Every morning there would be a line-up of people waiting to see Matron outside the hospital. Most of the regular patients lived in the old people's camp, coming in with tummy aches or infected sores. The weather was so hot and humid that the smallest pimple or sore would quickly turn into a giant-sized boil, and the threat of poisoned limbs was a real possibility.

One old fella had a bush name of Arobin that sounded a bit like aeroplane to white man's ears so, in mission style, he was often called Avro after Avro Anson planes. He lived out at the camp with his wife, who would dress him up before he came in to get his dressings changed. When I helped in the hospital that first time, he proudly walked up in his white shirt and loose trousers; he proudly bent over to show me the three boils on his backside and, once Matron had seen him, he walked out without his trousers on. I was such an innocent young thing that I wasn't sure whether to be shocked or to laugh. He was perfectly happy, and that was enough.

The stores in the hospital were pretty rudimentary: salts for stomach aches, Sloan's pain killer for rheumatism, Aspro for headaches and Golden Eye ointment for sore eyes. Boils were treated with poultices, Dettol and liniment. If anyone was really sick, we would try to get the Royal Flying Doctor Service to come out from Derby or, if the plane couldn't make it, the patient would be sent on the launch to Wyndham for treatment.

The main diet at the mission was bread and meat. For the first few days after a bullock was killed, the meals were all meat; then, until the next kill, if fresh vegetables weren't available, we had tinned fruit and vegetables—a small ration allocated to each person from the store. Every Saturday, the men would put on their red *nagas* (rectangular piece of cloth that goes between their legs and is tied at the hips), collect their spears, woomeras and boomerangs and go off hunting for the day. Their wives would have to collect wood and prepare for the return feast. If they were particularly success-ful with their hunt, the meat would be shared with us.

Louisa would often take the dormitory girls for a picnic, and I would sometimes go out with them. We would take a loaf of bread and come home very full, having caught and cooked fish and eaten wild melons, or whatever else was in season. Fresh vegetables came from our gardens or the vegetable plot, but they tended to be random, depending on the season and how much gardening had been done. At the start I was a bit concerned that the diet at Forrest River wouldn't boost my chances of staying healthy and was glad that I had brought along some multivitamins and salt tablets.

As the start of the school year was fast approaching, the school program was planned out and the lunches that would be cooked in the kitchen for all the school kids by Matron were organised. I fished through textbooks and other teaching resources that would suit all the year groups I would be teaching. There were plenty of resources that followed the educational curriculum, but some of them were a little worse for wear; the school had been going for many years prior to being taken over by the state education department. Everything was ready to go, but Lisa still hadn't arrived so, at Bill's request, I started the school year as the only teacher, in the knowledge that, when she did arrive, she could and probably would change everything.

4

FITTING IN

My first ever class numbered forty-five students, twice what would be considered a good-sized class these days, with the kids ranging in age from five to sixteen years. It was a lot of work, but we did it, and had a lot of fun.

The kids were thrilled with the idea of changing the words in English nursery rhymes that they already knew, to better suit where we were. We changed 'round and round the mulberry bush' to 'round and round the boab tree', and 'cold and frosty morning' to 'hot and dusty morning'. Later I would hear them being sung around the mission after school, mixed in with their own songs—our versions of these old rhymes were much better suited to a climate far removed from where they originated.

On my second day with them, I managed to settle all the kids down and was calmly reading them a story when they all seemed to jump up as one, raced outside and were pointing at the sky. They could hear a plane that was miles away. I hadn't heard a thing until we were outside. I learnt later it was the aerodrome inspector, coming out to check on the airstrip; but he didn't come into our compound.

The landing strip at Forrest River was used primarily by the Royal Flying Doctor Service for emergencies. That weekend there was a great flurry of excitement on hearing over the radio that a doctor would be visiting. We still had no nurse at the mission, so all the patients had to be taken the nearly one kilometre from the village to the airfield so a medical professional could assess their various ailments. With what seemed like only ten minutes' warning, a flurry of patients was collected from the hospital and various homes, and everything made ready at the strip. But, as we all stood and watched the plane, it flew over and headed off in the direction of Kulumburu, the northernmost settlement in the state.

After Bill contacted them on the radio, we were told they would call in on the way back in the afternoon, so all the preparations were repeated. But again they didn't stop. The next message from Wyndham said that even though the RFDS thought the pilot intended to stop, he was never going to because he had orders from Perth not to.

Father Coaldrake thought the orders not to land had come from MacRobertson Miller Airlines. Given my connections with the airline, through Dad, I was unpopular until they found out that the orders had come from the aerodrome inspector who had interrupted our class the week before. Apparently the inspector had reported that the strip was alright, but the grass was too long. Unfortunately that information hadn't been passed on to the mission and the grass hadn't been mown.

At about this time I was introduced to a beautiful baby boy whom they called Edwin Cyril—Cyril after my father. Dad was heavily involved with the Native Welfare Council and for many years was chair of this group of non-government organisations interested in Aboriginal welfare. He would often visit various Aboriginal communities in the North West and had visited Wyndham a few years before I arrived. The locals joked that the baby was Sister Gare's 'Dardy'. I still have a wonderful photo of me holding baby Cyril on my hip.

I was getting used to having so many kids at school, but it was hard work trying to keep them all interested, as they were at different levels and I couldn't concentrate on any one year group or student. I was really looking forward to having just the Infants and Years One and Two when Lisa eventually turned up.

I used to write home to my family at least once a week, sometimes more. It was usually a hurried note composed just before the launch was about to depart for Wyndham, though some nights I would make the time to write and reflect on the happenings at my new home, as well as send requests for things I thought I could use at the school.

It dawned on me fairly early that, as far as possible, the arrangements seemed to have been made so that the white staff were not left at each other's mercies too much. The idea seemed to be that when there are only a few white people around and they are thrown together, they are likely to get on each other's nerves. I didn't question this at the time, though I sometimes longed for some decent conversation. I felt alone, especially at night when I thought of home; to make matters worse, my feet started to swell up.

Forrest River was beautiful, and the Oombulgurri welcomed me, as I made an effort and cared. I wrote home that it was a carefree country where I was learning to live, laugh, be merry and stand on my own two feet. I was meeting people, talking with them about anything. Life was altogether different there; in fact, every day I thought I would like Perth less and less. The only drawbacks were human inflicted.

~

The following weekend Lisa and Connie arrived. Connie was about the same age as me and had trained and practised as a teacher, I think after attending a mission school in Alice Springs. She would be helping us at the school as a teaching assistant with the kindergarten-aged children and she was a lovely, bright young lady. Lisa, on the other hand, was less than impressed that I had already started the school year without her.

I found both Father and Mrs Coaldrake easy to get on with. I offered my services as an organist and Sunday School teacher, though I was finding the length of time in church on my knees rather painful. I was going nine times a week and, apart from the dormitory kids, who had to go, I was the only other regular attendee. Most of the village people went to church at Easter and Christmas or special occasions. It seemed that the only mission inhabitants who attended church did so because they had to. Father Coaldrake and I would have interesting religious discussions after church, which I enjoyed. I think I was even forgiven for being a Quaker.

I was getting plenty of visitors at my flat. It started off with the school kids coming to play with the marbles and jacks (knucklebones) that I had brought up with me. They had never seen them before. I only had to show them how to play once, and they loved it. The most popular toy at the mission was made from two tins filled with sand, wired together and attached to the end of a long stick. Some kids even had three or four tins wired together; they were happy pushing them around, the tins rattling over and through the dirt all day, with the kids making engine noises as they did so.

One of the local men, Crispin Mitchell, was a good artist and he painted a beautiful picture of the Wyndham hills for me. After he left, I put it into an old frame and hung it on the wall of my flat. When I told him what I had done, he was delighted. I was then visited by at least a dozen men; Crispin had told them to come and see his painting at Djidja Gare's house.

Some of the older girls came for a visit and saw some of my family photos and asked me everyone's names. Afterwards, whenever I saw them, they would repeat all of the names back to me with pride. I became friends with a seventeen-year-old girl, Gwen Morgan, who had left school the previous year and was working at the hospital. We'd often go for walks, then go back to her family home for supper. Her dad had built a chook yard and had a well-kept garden; they were great company, especially compared to the whites, who were still keeping mostly to themselves.

One night I had visits from Gwen, then her younger sister Miriam, her big brother Ken, followed by half a dozen men and seven mothers with babies and children. The fathers came in after they had separated some boys fighting outside. In my sitting room there was quite a bit of floor space, and we all happily sat around on the floor, which seemed to be alive with marbles, knucklebones, lizards, bugs, frogs and kids. The men were looking at the few magazines I had arrived with. Two of them were looking at a wildlife book Dad had given me before I left.

Then suddenly both of them jumped up with a yell. They had come across a picture of a snake. They told me that their blood runs cold at the sight of even the harmless ones. A poisonous snake is a 'cheeky fella', a great insult. A cheeky person was also someone too important, too stuck-up to be a part of a community. Apparently they thought Lisa was sometimes a cheeky person.

Whenever the kids came to visit my house, after school or on weekends, they'd all sit around on my floor. In one corner some would be drawing, some reading, some playing a drum or a mouth organ. In another corner, there would be a group turning nursery rhymes into corroboree songs. It was wonderful.

On Fridays I would go out and watch public corrobborees or ceremonies, as some people like to now call them, at the old people's camp. The men would be painted for special dances and would often make special props. They made up dances about happenings inside and outside the mission.

There was one created by the neighbouring Drysdale Aboriginal people about the *Koolinda*, the old cargo and passenger steamship that had travelled up and down the Western Australian coast for many decades. For this one it took two old men all day to wind wool around some wooden frames to represent sails. They were spectacular. During the dance, the nappy of the baby I was holding was whisked off for one of the dancers to wear. Throughout these performances, there would always be dogs fighting and babies crying.

By my second visit I knew how to do the dance of the brolgas and beat rhythm sticks. The Oombulgurri were all very excited about the dances and songs, especially when an old man put in a few extra movements in the wild turkey dance. This was a lively dance, in contrast to another that I was quietly told dealt with the soggy bread that Matron had been cooking for us staff members. I'm not sure that this was true, but all of them had been joking about it and feeling sorry for me having to eat it. The dance was slow and heavy. The words of the song sounded very like 'doughy, doughy'. That did make me smile. Poor Matron—good thing she wasn't there.

~

The Sunday after the *Koolinda* dance, the stockman Harold Weibye and I had a lesson in spear throwing. The men almost did a dance right then and there, when on my first try I managed to throw a spear using the woomera. I must admit I was pretty chuffed, but that soon changed.

My next lesson was cracking a stockwhip. I finished up being only able to make a feeble noise; I had many red marks on my arms and legs and I became tangled in it. It wasn't until I had been going for nearly twenty minutes that they brought out another stockwhip. The one I had been using was only for the men to show off with; it was incredibly long and heavy. I knew I would be very stiff and sore the next day at school.

I finished up the day by trying to ride a horse in a circle, but I couldn't even get it to move until one of the boys helped me by leading it. They all thought it was a great joke to see someone being led—even the little kids could ride by themselves.

I was living in just the three dresses that I had packed in my suitcase, as I was still waiting for my big box of belongings and hand-powered sewing machine to arrive from Perth. To make room for books, magazines, my sewing kit, marbles and knucklebones, I hadn't packed many clothes, thinking the rest of my belongings would arrive shortly after me. Everything delivered to Wyndham had to come out on the little mission launch. Having no set schedule, it only went when it was needed. For three weeks it went in about twice a week, but then the following week not at all.

I had to go back into Wyndham on the launch, my first trip after arriving, as my swollen feet turned out to be the result of infected mosquito bites. The glands in my groin were now swollen and sore, so I needed to go in for a series of penicillin injections. I learnt a big lesson—don't scratch mosquito bites!

It was lovely to see the river and gulf in daylight. I remember seeing a big white-faced crocodile smiling at me with its open mouth from the bank, a herd of cattle and loads of donkeys. Plenty of mullet skimmed across the surface as a summer storm started to brew up above the cliff tops. The trip out and back seemed to take days, not hours, so different and so much to see in the daylight. My box still hadn't arrived, but there were some very welcome parcels from my parents.

Mum and Dad had sent fresh lemons for head colds, which, in my letters, I had told them abounded in the kids. Then I promptly caught a cold myself. They also sent vegetable and flower seeds for the garden I planned; clothing for the kids; material for new clothes. Also some precious photos I had taken in the first couple of weeks at the mission and which had now been developed. There were things I'd requested for the kids: more marbles, balls, tennis racquets, plus different coloured papers and materials for the school, for which I reimbursed them from my wages with a posted cheque.

When I first arrived, the dormitory girls only seemed to have one pair of pants and two dresses—one for school and dinner, the other for other times. They joked about the time when they would have pyjamas *and* slippers *and* dressing gowns. I asked my parents to hunt out any clothes and fabrics they could find to send, also towels and handkerchiefs, as well as socks to keep foot dressings in place at the hospital. Everything at the mission was patched, even curtains and bedspreads, because getting replacements was not easy or even possible.

I had brought a camera up with me and it was trial and error with the first few rolls of film I used, followed by a long wait to see the prints. I would send the rolls of film down to Perth, where Mum and Dad would get them processed for me, and then the prints would make the long trip back. They were hugely exciting to share with everyone when they returned. The Oombulgurri all loved seeing the photos, especially when there was someone in them that they knew.

Many of the women wore dresses made out of bleached flourbags, so I was absolutely delighted when my big box and hand-powered sewing machine finally arrived. I always took great pride in sewing my own clothes and enjoyed sewing with the other women at Forrest River. I had been gifted a little sewing caddy that I treasured from a remarkable lady, Mollie Skinner. Through her work, Mollie had inspired me as a teenager to work with Aboriginal people.

I first met Mollie at a Quaker meeting with my parents. You'd see her in the village and ask how she was, and she'd always reply, 'Oh, as ugly as ever!' At meetings, I remember her hearing aids used to squeal, which made us 'Young Friends' giggle. She'd been born with a cleft palate, and as a young girl, while at boarding school in England, she developed ulcerated corneas, which they used to treat with cocaine drops. These, in turn, badly scarred her eyes. She went on to train as a nurse and midwife in England; she then worked in India and Burma during the First World War before coming to Perth, where she established hospitals in the country towns of Wagin and Katanning. She achieved all of this when, by today's standards, she'd be classified as legally blind.

Her last nursing job was during the Second World War, working at the Moore River Aboriginal Settlement, where she was much loved. She was a remarkable woman and is credited with starting the Quakers' interest in Aboriginal people, through the Australian Aboriginal League. Later, when she knew I was to be a teacher, she, along with my parents, encouraged me to work with Aboriginal kids. I thought of her whenever I used that little caddy. Unfortunately she passed away the year before I left for Forrest River, but it was her modesty, courage, hard work and personal integrity that I knew her best for, and aspired to.

Along with my big box and sewing machine, more clothing had arrived, donated by Quaker Friends and people we knew. The airline donated some old hostess uniforms and Perth

(Ladies) College provided old school uniforms for the older girls and ladies to wear.

The dormitory girls loved the fashionable fabrics and clothing coming up from Perth, even if they were a few seasons old. Every delivery felt like Christmas.

5

FINDING INSPIRATION

After Lisa arrived, the school kids were split into their two class groups. I had the younger ones, and Lisa had the Years Three to Six group. The kids in my younger classes were so affectionate, wanting hugs every morning before sitting down at their desks. The kids in one group would be seated with their backs to those in the other group, and Lisa and I would face each other, each with a blackboard behind us.

Not only could we see what our kids were doing, but each other as well, which was a little distracting and disconcerting both for me and my kids. I decided to take my kids outside for lessons whenever I could. Both they and I appreciated it, and they were keen to count, sing and do activities in the open air, where they were so much happier.

I remembered clearly from my own primary school days when our teacher once took us outside and asked us to make a great big pile of dirt and then randomly placed rocks of all sizes in it. He then brought over a watering can and sprinkled the water on top to show us what happens on bare dirt when it rains. We saw rivers and creeks form, flowing past the random rocks in the soil, and ending as a big puddle at the bottom. It was such a great explanation of geology and then geography as he showed us how an Indian delta worked, and it all stuck with me. It was my sort of teaching—raising kids' curiosity and increasing their desire to learn. While outside, we would pick up things to count, put in order and name, learning and enjoying ourselves at the same time.

At school Lisa was very strict and always walked around her students with a cane in her hand. Even then, sixty-odd years ago, at teachers' college we were taught that if you hit a child, you had failed. I was determined that I was not going to hit any child at all, even though my superior was convinced that the Oombulgurri kids needed strict discipline.

I remember saying something about the amount of physical fighting that went on in the playground and someone replied, 'Oh, that's just in their culture.' That's how it was, and it was accepted. I didn't like accepting it but, being young and inexperienced, I did. It was my way of fitting in with the whites. The kids were lovely, but they did physically fight with each other a lot.

Thinking about it at the time, I put it down to the fact that they had experienced white influence for so long; that they also knew the stories of Reverend Gribble and his stockwhip, together with the history of the massacre. The Rev Ernest Gribble used to keep discipline within the mission with a stockwhip that he apparently kept with him at all times. I wasn't aware of this when I began teaching there but, as time went on, it explained a few things.

There was no drinking alcohol and no drugs in those days. Forrest River was a dry mission, and yet there was a lot of fighting among the adults, some of them needing to be patched up at the hospital afterwards. They played cards at night and usually the fighting was over gambling. There was a bright red satin shirt that would be wagered; it would change hands just about every night. They played a card game where you had to add the cards up to ten; they knew every combination of numbers from one to ten. Even the little kids knew how to count; for them it was great fun.

Lisa was very critical of me for associating with the Oombulgurri, and at school she was pretty tough. She had told me that as long as I did a good job with teaching, she wouldn't care what I did outside of school hours. Yet she cared enough to regularly tell me and all the staff that, although I was doing a good job in school, I was too much of a chicken to be on a mission, where life was hard. That I had led too much of a sheltered life to truly understand human nature, which was probably true in some ways. But by far the thing she disliked most was that I was too friendly with all the people. When dealing with her, and to help me get through, I often thought of Kath Skipsey, one of the most inspirational people I had known in my short years.

~

Kath had moved with her husband and two children to Darlington, the little village where we lived outside of Perth, during the Second World War. When Mum found out she had run two different Girl Guide companies, she asked Kath about starting a Girl Guide company for girls over eleven years, my age at the time.

Kath, or 'Cap' as we came to call her, agreed. I remember that from then on, I lived for the Saturday afternoon Girl Guides meetings; I enjoyed the games and hearing about all the camps and activities we were going to have. Cap must have spent ages preparing for those meetings because I remember them being very exciting—always a great mix of games, skills, moral teaching and formality. The theme was always international, to develop a feeling of belonging to a large multinational and multicultural world. This was very much in alignment with my father's views and, by default, mine. She sent some of us off to a camp in Perth with a contingent of Guides who had come out from Malaya, and I attended an International Jamboree in Sydney in 1951.

I did love Guides and truly loved the international aspect of it. To go over to Sydney for the International Jamboree, I competed for a scholarship. I remember trying out with a whole heap of Guides from all over the state. I knew I was coming first after the first test, and I got a bit of a shock. It was a cooking test, and I managed to successfully cook an egg inside a jacket potato on a campfire. We were tested on first aid and all sorts of other skills, but I know it was the general knowledge of the world test, the bit on geography, that let me down. I ended up coming third and was awarded a partial scholarship. Even though we didn't have much money, Dad managed to get enough together to pay for the remainder of the costs; he knew how much interaction we'd have with Guides from other nations.

Cap wasn't a bossy or domineering leader but a very gentle and dignified lady, who was fun loving and attracted respect without demanding it. She was always welcoming to Guides, who visited her often during the week to get help with some badge. She helped and inspired us to pass all the tests and challenges.

With her help and encouragement, I earned the Queen's Guide Award, the ultimate test, when I was just fifteen. The Queen's Guide award was the highest attainable in the Guide movement. I had to complete an individual project, and then had to tackle a series of tests. You had to be prepared; there were often surprises associated with Guide tests, and we learnt to use our initiative.

I remember one test I had was to catch a train to Perth and find a house in Cottesloe that sat on stilts. The person there pretended to have a sprained ankle, so I used my necktie as a bandage, and the two pennies I always had in my pocket to make a telephone call then came into use. A Guide always had part of a matchbox with the striker, two matches, two pennies and a needle and thread in her pocket and wore a triangular necktie—to be prepared for just about anything.

I think my award was one of the last signed by the Queen Mother; with the young Princess Elizabeth, herself a Guide, coming onto the throne, I became a little obsessed with all things royal for a period. I would collect newspaper and magazine articles, especially about the 1952 royal visit to Australia. Anything relating to the good in them, their good deeds, something to aspire to and be proud of.

Guides and Kath Skipsey certainly taught me to be confident. Even now, when faced with a daunting challenge, I can hear Kath say, 'You can do it! You're a Queen's Guide!'

To me, of the ten Guide Laws, the law that Cap embodied most was that 'A Guide smiles and sings under all difficulties'.

She had the shiniest white teeth I had ever seen; whenever I think of her now, I see her beautiful smiling face. In some of the most difficult periods in my life, I would think of Cap and this particular law, and just smile and sing my way through. It certainly helped me at times with Lisa. I took her criticism hard, but smiled and sang my way through it—mostly Oombulgarri songs, much to Lisa's horror.

6

GUIDES

The only time I stood up to Lisa at Forrest River was during the first term, when I thought the girls would benefit from me starting a Girl Guide company. Lisa told me I would be too busy with school preparation—and she was too busy; she didn't like anything happening that she wasn't involved in. I felt she didn't trust me and, knowing how much I personally had gained from being a Guide, I was eager to share that experience with the older girls.

Bill took me aside and told me that he would support my idea; then he went and had a quiet word with Lisa. By the end of March, I had received approval from the mission's administrative committee in faraway Perth and I felt so happy, I wanted to smile and sing out of pure happiness. Connie was going to help me, and I was even more delighted to find that Sheila Hill, our new nurse who would be arriving shortly at the mission, was also a Guider. In fact, I knew her! I had met her at Guide leader's conferences back in Perth—such a small world.

I started thinking about which girls would be good leaders, and how I would organise uniforms and equipment. I truly didn't care that any free time I had would now be gone. As well as teaching, preparing classes, tending my garden, taking Sunday School and playing the organ in church, I would also have Guides every Saturday. I have always preferred to be busy.

We started Guides without uniforms or much equipment but, as the kids were used to going out most weekends, camping wasn't new to them. They'd take me out into the bush, and we'd sit beside the river eating wild melons, talking about Guides and planning things to learn, ways to earn badges. I showed them how to make dough with self-raising flour and water and wrap it around a green stick to cook over a campfire, a slow process to make sure the dough was cooked through without turning the outside to charcoal. Once cooked, we slid them off the stick and filled them with golden syrup—delicious, though a tad messy.

We divided the Guides into three families, Wattles, Black Cockatoos (*Wulgnas*) and *Munumburras* (the name of the launch), but this patrol later changed its name to Brolgas (*Grondas*). At this early stage, none of the girls wanted purely Aboriginal names, because 'they sound silly'. I thought that was a great pity, but it was no good trying to force them.

The girls were being influenced by magazines that were coveted among them—full of gossip about movie stars and the latest trends. At school I'd encourage the singing of the songs that we'd sing out at the old people's camp and ask them to teach me their language, but the older kids were often more interested in what was happening in the outside world, away from their own culture. I was excited, however, that the girls seemed to enjoy Guides as much as I did, and the hunt was now on for fabric to make enough uniforms.

There was another source of excitement. The Western Australian government was running what were known as the North West Camp Schools in Perth for kids, both Aboriginal and non-Aboriginal, from schools in the North West of Western Australia. Three or four kids from each school would be flown down for two weeks of exploring and education, staying in dormitories at Point Peron, at what I think was an old navy base. The Education Department telegrammed, asking for one of the Forrest River teachers to accompany the FRM kids and the kids from Wyndham.

Without any discussion, Lisa said she was going. I would have loved to have been at the camp, but part of me actually didn't want to go. I knew that after it was over, I would have had to endure farewelling my family in Perth again. Given my homesickness, I might not have come back!

The camp school was planned for two weeks in early April and I was excited for the three Forrest River kids who were going. They were a jolly fine bunch. I remember worrying they would probably be shy and bewildered by it all to begin with. But I shouldn't have worried—kids being kids, they all got on famously.

Tensions among the staff bubbled below the surface each day. Many were unhappy, particularly Connie, who wanted to leave. She wasn't the only one. Matron O'Reilly was leaving with her son, and then Father Coaldrake handed in his resignation after many years at the mission, all within the same month. Matron and her son left almost immediately, and the Coaldrakes would leave when a replacement was found. They'd all had enough.

7

BEATEN

I had been brought up a pacifist by my parents. After the First World War my dad had been concerned about the violence that we humans inflicted on each other; so much so that, at the start of the Second World War, he registered as a conscientious objector.

Dad, at this time, was also troubled religiously. He could not in good conscience recite the Church of England Nicene Creed, the one that starts: *I believe in God, the father almighty, maker of heaven and earth, and in Jesus Christ, his only son, Our Lord, Born of the Virgin Mary.* He could not say it with any honest conviction. He didn't believe in miracles; he was just a positive, logical thinker, rather than theological. He looked for the good in people, and the world.

Dad became a pacifist and, even though we were practising members of the Church of England at the time, he started investigating other religious denominations. This was very hard on Mum, whose brother Ralph was a Church of England parson. I remember one religious group Dad was looking into forbade women from cutting their hair. I saw Mum crying on the wood heap about that one. Poor Mum.

Dad's registration as a conscientious objector came to a head on 9 September 1942, when he and six other men had to appear at a special court hearing in Perth. Dad told the court that while he thought the Bible was the greatest collection of books in history, he did not believe in interpreting it literally, and that it was his ideal to bring up his family based on a life of pacifism. A canon from the Church of England vouched for Dad's sincerity in his belief, and the magistrate reserved his decision for four weeks.

It was a tough month of waiting, for Mum especially. Gaol was a real possibility; many conscientious objectors had already been sent there. On the day of the decision, I remember Dad kissing Mum in the kitchen at home; he tried to lighten the mood by telling her, 'I'll let you know when visiting hours will be,' before he headed out the door to court. Thankfully, the magistrate decided that Dad was a sincere conscientious objector. Some thought this decision was because Dad's work with the airlines was more useful to the war effort than him being a soldier.

Dad strongly believed in equality and peace, working for better living standards and for Aboriginal people to integrate rather than be assimilated. Many years later his work with the Quakers and Australian Aboriginal people sent him to the United Nations. He and Mum lived and worked in New York for three months.

I agreed with his views on peace, and classified myself as a pacifist, but that was about to be sorely tested.

~

Fights in the village were common and discipline in the homes was violent, sometimes carried out with a stockwhip, mostly by husbands on wives, or jealous wives on each other. Tempers seemed to fly up and down very quickly, and I often blamed the weather.

It was now early autumn and it was still about 105 degrees Fahrenheit (forty degrees Celsius) from ten in the morning until six at night, hot and muggy. Even with nightfall, it didn't cool down much until about two in the morning. Thankfully the rain had almost gone, though there were still thunderstorms and thick cloud around.

While Lisa was away with the North West camp kids, I had all the students again, which was exhausting and at times became tense. The kids, like everyone, loved their freedom and independence. The mission aimed to get as many kids as possible to high school, and the general plan was that they had to be taught concern for others and not to strike out at each other.

While Lisa was away, they refused to do some things for me, especially the older boys. They would shout at each other and put up their fists, often taking a swing or two at each other, then ten minutes later they were all love and kisses again. But I was concerned at the damage they could do to each other, and to me, when their tempers went off. My responsibility for the whole school during those two weeks stretched my non-violent principles almost to breaking point. On one occasion all my mighty muscles had to be deployed to hold on to one boy who had lost his temper. I was considering taking up ju-jitsu!

One of the biggest lessons I learnt during my time at Forrest River was that violence breeds violence. I am ashamed to say that following an incident that occurred after Lisa's return with the camp kids, I could no longer call myself a non-violent teacher.

Henry Umbulgurri was a big eleven-year-old and a troubled child with a vile temper. One time previously he had almost pushed Lisa off a cliff edge in anger. In class one day, I rapped his knuckles, and he stood up and raised his fists at me in a threatening manner. When Lisa saw this, she came and gave him a sound caning, then he received nothing short of a thrashing from his father that afternoon after school. I felt dreadful.

That night he walked up to my place and put his arm around me and played games on the floor with the other kids. I don't think he played up because he didn't like me; it was the discipline he resented. When the kids were outside and at home, they could get out of most things by lashing out.

After that one incident I never hit a student again, especially after I'd listened and watched some of the smallest girls playing schools and giving their version of classroom discipline, rapping each other's knuckles, walking around with a stick, and pulling ears. They showed me how childish it was. In fact, I think I only carried a rod or short cane in class for what would be less than two weeks, but I was dreadfully ashamed that I had hit someone. Never again. There were better ways to create an interest in learning.

I was happy that three of my five infant-grade students were reading well; of the other two, one six-year-old was trying hard and the other, who was aged eight, had problems talking and didn't have a care in the world. We had a new enrolment halfway through the term—Stephen, a five-year-old child who had been sent to us from Wyndham, where he'd been found wandering around the hospital, calling himself 'King Stephen'. His surname could have been King, or he could have been related to King Peter, the head of the Oombulgurri in Wyndham.

I have no idea what had happened to his parents. Stephen didn't care for discipline and had little interest in schoolwork; if things were quiet, I'd often see him outside playing. It was easy to win his interest, so we did even more lessons outside and I made them as interesting and relevant to their lives as I could, giving Stephen little jobs to do to help.

When I'd been doing prac. teaching at teachers' college, one of my first placements had been at Thomas Street School, right next to the Perth Modern School. I'd had plenty of fun, especially with the mischievous ones. One boy couldn't seem to concentrate for more than five minutes and made a real nuisance of himself. When I made him feel important—I gave him the job of messenger boy, and extra help with his work—he started to thrive in class. He also showed great disappointment with himself when he had to be 'spoken to'. Before I left, he was singing the song I taught in class, something he had never done before.

This was a tactic I would use into the future with disruptive pupils and adults as I went through life. Talk with them, make them feel important, involved and useful. It works. So that was the approach I took to Forrest River and beyond; to me it was preferable to hitting out.

Some kids weren't strong in certain subjects we taught, but they were in others. To me that was the strength I wanted to find in them, despite Lisa's insistence that they be good at all subjects.

8

CHEEKY SNAKES

I regularly attended church and, as the church was open on all four sides, snakes were quite a common occurrence, causing many shrieks and uproar when one wound itself around the rafters. During one well-attended evening service, I was reverently kneeling when I heard a whisper from the men across the aisle, 'Sister, Sister!' Although I couldn't see what they were pointing at, I knew from their faces it must be a snake. They seemed to be pointing at my feet, so I managed to jump and land, still on my knees, in front of where I'd been kneeling. Turning back, I saw a small snake slithering off down the aisle, quickly followed by Tenny, who chased and trod on it behind its head, before picking it up and taking it outside.

I turned to the wide-eyed men who had warned me; they were still frozen on the spot. Afterwards they joked with me that they thought it was using my dress as a kneeling mat and saying its prayers with me! It had been small, but it was nonetheless of the venomous variety.

With the Dry Season settling in, as well as the snakes that would appear in the dry grass, dusty willy-willies were regular occurrences. I asked my parents to send up more flower and vegetable seeds, as gardening seemed to keep the willy-willies down. I seemed to be asking them to send up a lot of things, but I could see so much that could be done if only we had the resources.

Friends sent second-hand children's books, which were great both for school and when the kids visited me. A little primus stove was also sent up for me. I loved the freedom that small gift provided—I could make myself hot drinks in my room without having to traipse down to the kitchen at night. A thoughtful gift indeed.

After a quiet start to the Easter weekend at the mission, with only four village fights, the church on Sunday was full. It was my first experience of a High Church Easter. The church had been decorated with tree branches and zinnias and there was a procession of men and boys in red coats and white cassocks. Peter Coaldrake, who was all of about five years of age, looked quite comical walking beside a tall man who was swinging the incense, who must have been about six foot four inches (193 centimetres) tall.

Everything was bright, everyone was happy. The smell of the incense and the freshly cut gum-tree boughs overpowered the usually sour, musty smell in the church walls that still lingered from the Wet Season. In muggy weather, even our clean clothes started to smell sour.

Quite a few Wyndham people, both Aboriginal and non-Aboriginal, came to the mission for the Easter service, as there wasn't a Church of England church in Wyndham at that time. I would be involved in the opening of that many years later. The Aboriginal visitors joined in the hunting, fishing and ceremonies that followed.

The atmosphere of the day was only dampened by Lisa, who accused everyone of being hollow, because they didn't regularly attend church and yet had enjoyed the service. When I tried to join in the religious discussion, she turned on me with, 'Wait till you've travelled around a bit. You're nothing but a babe in napkins [nappies] and that's straight!' I nearly laughed, but everyone else was quiet.

Bill and Mary thought that she might have upset me, and told me not to worry about her childish behaviour. I could see she was a good woman, trying her best, but it wasn't my fault, as far as I could see, that she didn't seem to like me.

9

MOUNT HOUSE STATION

There were three school terms a year back then, not four like now, with one lot of school holidays in May and the other in September. By the May school holidays, Dad had organised for me to visit the Blythe family, whom he knew through his MMA connections and a company called Air Beef. Air Beef had been formed to transport beef quickly, using MMA, initially from the remote Blythe station, Glenroy in the West Kimberley, on to major markets. To put cattle on the road and walk them meant they would lose condition, and it was time consuming. An abattoir and chilling centre were built at Glenroy, and thousands of tonnes of chilled beef were flown from the West Kimberley to Perth, Singapore and Asia. With me being in the area, he must have asked Mr Blythe if I could visit during the school holidays.

The mission launch broke down on the night we were supposed to leave, and it didn't look as though we would get away in time for me to catch the plane from Wyndham to Derby, to connect with the Air Beef plane. Thankfully Bill and Bob Morrow worked at night, at low tide, and managed to get the old girl going again.

It was pretty hot out on the open launch, and my poor fair skin took a good blast despite it being almost winter. The trip took all day in the full sun. I stayed at the hotel that night, ready to catch the morning flight. Even though it was the night before the Wyndham races, I had a relatively peaceful sleep.

Having flown out in the morning, I then sat at Derby waiting for the Air Beef plane, which was due to fly out at 1 p.m. By the time 4 p.m. came around, although I wasn't worried, I was curious as to whether I'd been forgotten or not. The plane did finally arrive, however, with a new pilot from India, who told me he had to go into town and get beer for a party. So we jumped into an old MMA ute at the aerodrome. But it wouldn't start, so I had to get out and push, jumping back in when the engine spluttered to life. When we stopped at the pub, the handbrake wouldn't work. With the ute parked on a slope outside the pub, I sat with my foot on the brake pedal while the beer was purchased and loaded in.

The ute started this time, and we took off back to the aerodrome in a mighty rush, as it was starting to get dark. We loaded the beer and the other supplies that were going out to the station, tying it all down with ropes, and at last took off on the 170-kilometre trip. I stood behind the pilot during the flight and looked out into the dwindling light; he kindly explained to me all of the controls and what he was doing, which I found fascinating.

We landed at Glenroy just on nightfall. The governess, a lovely young lady called Beverley, opened my door. She was accompanied by an Aboriginal man and a mob of kids who surrounded her. They all quickly piled into the plane, undoing ropes and heaving crates out and into a ute. There was a rush of hasty introductions from Bev as she lumped a bag of sugar over her shoulder and carried a crate of beer. I grabbed what I could and helped, stumbling in the dim light.

When everything was loaded into the waiting ute, we jumped in and I managed to have the door slammed on my foot. Then we sped to the end of the runway so we could beam the ute's lights back down it so the pilot could take off in the dark and fly back to Derby.

There were six white kids at the station—the three that Bev schooled plus three visitors for the holidays—and they all shouted instead of talked. Mealtimes were total bedlam, but great fun.

The following morning Mr Blythe took me for a tour of the abattoir so I could see the entire process, from killing to loading. I even packed a few parcels of rump steak, though I was a bit concerned that I might have left them a bit loose and they might be frosted by the time they arrived in Perth.

Next, we went out to kill a beast for station meat. The stockmen and butchers mustered a herd and stood back as the boss shot 'the killer', then they all helped to skin and cut it up. I had a lot of fun talking with the Aboriginal stockmen; some of the older ones knew Oombulgurri people who had visited Derby for medical treatment or to visit relatives and friends. Although their language wasn't quite the same, some of the words were similar and I was accepted as a friend straight away when I spoke a few words in Oombulgurri.

The following day Mr Blythe took me on a drive around Glenroy and the homestead; we stayed for a movie at the meatworks that night, before driving to the neighbouring Blythe property, Mount House Station, by ute the following day.

One memory of that visit sticks strongly in my mind. I was by the river with Bev, while the six white kids she was looking after were running around with the Aboriginal kids, and she asked me how I felt about her teaching just the white kids, when the Aboriginal kids didn't get educated. I think I told her that I would have loved to teach them all. I also remember one white woman being shocked that I would take the time to talk to the Aboriginal women who worked at the homestead, and she told me so in no uncertain terms. After that I tried to avoid all conversations about 'natives' and missions during the rest of my stay, because I didn't want to upset my hosts.

We went mustering every day and I rode a nineteen-year-old horse called Scooby and loved it. From that day on, I wanted to marry a Nor-West man and live that life forever.

For the last few days of my visit, we camped at a gorge about forty-five kilometres from Mount House. Despite its beauty, the most amazing thing to me was the fact that I'd ridden out that far on poor old Scooby. We had camped at a stock camp on the way there and we swam and fished and slid down long, sloping waterfalls, before making it back in time for me to catch the Air Beef plane back to Wyndham. Years later Bev told me that after I flew out, Scooby left the homestead and cleared off, never to be seen again. It must have all been too much for the old fellow.

It had been the best holiday, just what I needed, and I was grateful to the Blythe family for welcoming me and showing me their life. It was certainly a welcome break away from the turmoil among the staff at Forrest River.

By the time I caught the launch back to the mission, I was thankful that it was night; I sat in the dark as far away from the crew as possible. The engine was making a lot of noise, so I let myself have a good cry as we approached the mission, a real sob with noise and tears flowing freely. My first term had been hard, so what was the rest of my two years going to be like?

10

BISHOP AND JOHNNY

The Church of England bishop for the massive Nor-West region, Bishop Frewer, arrived for a visit at Forrest River. He told me he knew both my father and grandfather from when he had been a 'Bush Brother' in the days when the Gare family all lived in Katanning in southern Western Australia. He was known to all throughout the vast north, as he lived out of a suitcase, constantly travelling from one small town to another and from one station homestead and mining community to another, administering to his spread-out flock. He would travel using whatever transport was available, a lot by air. I think he accumulated over a thousand flights during his time in the North West, quite a feat at the time. He eventually received a Gold Pass from MMA so he could travel free of charge.

Whenever he visited, he seemed to enjoy himself in his somewhat eccentric way. On this visit, Bill and Mary woke up to hear trees falling. Old as he was—I think Bishop would have been in his late seventies by this stage—he couldn't bear to see dead trees or ones with pests in them, so down they came. I liked him, everyone did, and he was called Bishop or Bish. Bill said that he had 'cottoned on to me', so it seemed that I had again been forgiven for being a Quaker. We would have many visits from Bishop during my time at FRM, and all of them enjoyable. The kids and all the people loved him, so much so that it was decided that the new community hall being built at the mission would be named after him, Frewer Hall.

The Coaldrakes left not long after this, and their departure after so many years at the mission was long and sad. Even poor Sheila, who had only known them a short time, couldn't talk to anyone without crying. The old camp people had a long wailing session, and down at the boat even Keith (Father Coaldrake) was crying as he was saying goodbye. He usually appeared so tough, as if nothing could hurt him, but his tears flowed freely.

The entire mission was quiet the following day, but it was about to be livened up, on the return of the launch, with the arrival of our new matron, Mrs Johnson. I was excited to hear she was an old hand at teaching horse riding, so perhaps she could improve my riding skills. She was originally from New Zealand but told me she had actually spent eight weeks in Katanning, where my parents had grown up, and we knew some of the same people. I thought she was great, as long as you looked past the habitual cigarette, the jockey cap she wore all the time and her bulging shorts or slacks. She never ever seemed to wear a skirt, which was unusual for women at the time.

We missed the Coaldrakes. I especially missed Keith and his sensible, tolerant religious discussions. I hated to think what his son Peter would have thought of the new matron; he used to tell all smokers that they were dirty. With no minister on the place, the men, both Oombulgurri and white, took it in turns to take the service. The church attendance shot up. One night everyone on the mission except the camp people came to church. It was led by two of the men from the community and the sermon was relevant to their everyday life. I remember there was a lot of loud, enthusiastic singing at that service.

Matron—or Johnny, as she liked to be called—plus Sheila and her eight-year-old daughter, Elizabeth, all moved into the Coaldrakes' old house and were keen gardeners, despite the plagues of wild donkeys and goats that, given half a chance, headed straight for anything growing. The wild donkeys were now a real menace, more than they had ever been up to then. I remember the men went out and shot eighty donkeys one weekend, and then sixty the next.

I decided I was going to get a rifle for myself. Dad had always been a keen competition rifle shooter and had taught us how to shoot rabbits in the Hills district behind Perth as kids. He had won three King's Prizes for shooting and even went to England to represent Australia in 1928, but he gave up all competitive shooting when he became a pacifist and the army became involved with rifle clubs.

On Dad's recommendation I purchased a Lithgow .22, which I then took with me every time I went out of the mission. I could obtain fresh meat, and it was an escape from staff tensions. Matron and Lisa hadn't hit it off terribly well.

11

CHANGE OF SEASON

I would go on fishing or hunting trips most weekends after church with the Oombulgurri, usually travelling in the back of the mission truck. When we got to a fresh waterway, all the women and girls would walk along the creek banks, dragging wire netting. If they found a good patch of fish, along with the spears thrown by the men, people would be flying around everywhere. Sometimes I thought it would be safer to be a fish!

It was great fun, though I was wary about grabbing any big fish. I was told not to worry, as their fins don't stick into you and they didn't bite, but the size of some of the barramundi was something else. It beat me how these little girls could grab a twenty-pound (nine kilo) barramundi, stick their fingers through its gills and throw it up onto the bank.

We'd often see wild turkeys, brolgas and plenty of donkeys as the men chased goannas through the bush and into the water. For eating, goanna meat beats chicken any day. A bit tough to chew, but it isn't dry like white chicken meat can be.

With the Dry Season upon us, I started up a garden at the front of our house on stilts. This not only kept me busy but would eventually produce wonderful flowers and produce. The chilli plants and watermelons, in particular, took off. Both would occasionally be pinched by the kids—the melons for eating and the chillis for playing tricks on one another!

As the seasons changed, my hands seemed to be having some sort of reaction to the blackboard chalk. Who ever heard of a 'chalky', a teacher, being allergic to chalk? I had a red prickly rash all over both hands; all along my fingers there were small blisters that popped and peeled for nearly three weeks. Both Matron and Sheila came to the conclusion that it was from the chalk and asked the doctor in Wyndham to send out some allergy creams and tablets.

That was the only downside in my life. I could see that the work we were doing was helping the Oombulgurri—they were receiving healthcare, were sheltered and fed, and the kids were being educated while still able to be involved with their culture. There really was more good happening at the mission than bad, if only the staff could get on with each other. My kids were enjoying school, and Lisa and I were working together reasonably well, each teaching in our own way.

The general attitude in my class, I felt, was friendly and progressive, although the kids were not neat. I wanted to let them think for themselves and concentrate on what they were writing about without worrying about where they crossed their t's or whether their letters sloped in the right direction. Lisa thought this was not good enough, and she would periodically come down to our end of the room and knock their heads together. It made no difference, because they were working for me, not her.

The Guides were flourishing. I showed the girls photos of what a Guide uniform looked like, and they were most excited that they too would have them, if only I could find the material. Johnny told me she had some friends who wanted to buy all the material for the Guide uniforms. With much excitement I wrote to them, thanking them wholeheartedly for their generosity. I also heard from Guide headquarters that there was an English Guide trainer visiting the Northern Territory. I invited her to the mission and, after many letters back and forth, she was coming.

Miss Colvin arrived in the middle of July, and threw herself into helping Matron with the cooking, and helping me with the Guides. It was one of the biggest thrills of my young life when she enrolled my first six Guides under an enormous spreading boab tree at Daddaway, with most at the mission in attendance.

We had all behaved ourselves while Miss Colvin visited, but after her departure, tensions overflowed. It was as though everyone, Oombulgurri and white, had been holding everything in until she left. The heat returned, and we were swamped with mosquitoes and insects, attacking any uncovered skin, further irritating us all. Lisa was all but sent packing by Bill for her behaviour to staff; she only saved herself with an apology.

I'd also had enough of Lisa and how she was treating Connie, me and the kids. I really didn't know if I could stand another year of the situation. But I didn't want to leave the kids, their families and everything I had started, so I made up my mind that I wanted to continue to be a teacher there, and nothing was going to stop me. I smiled and kept going.

Then there was a huge fight, with three dormitory girls coming to blows over one boy. A fourteen-year-old girl had been stirring up trouble for a while. Bill gave her a thrashing with a strap, and all hell broke loose among the staff.

Sheila and Johnny were ardent disbelievers in corporal punishment and made a deputation to Bill the following day. Of course, I didn't, and still don't, agree with violence. Johnny had a BA in Psychology and told Bill that she had previously worked on a mission and had also been a schoolteacher. She was very sure of her grounds and Bill took quite a bit of notice of her. Sheila took the opportunity to tell off Lisa, insisting she stop hitting the students' heads and pulling their ears. Lisa only laughed at her and became more unbearable than ever.

Bill was a diabetic, and the following week he had to go to Wyndham to 'have his sugar fixed up'. He left handyman Bob in charge, but then Bob accidentally inhaled too much DDT dust at work and made himself sick. From there, things rapidly went further downhill.

Lisa disagreed with everyone, hitting my kids left and right, as well as her own. She finally blew up and one night decided not to eat with us. Johnny told her where she could get her food, which would be dished out separately, and Lisa took a swing at her with a torch. Johnny then grabbed Lisa's arm and brought her over to face everyone.

Lisa shouted, used bad language and let rip. Pointing at each one of us in turn, she asked us if we liked her; if not, why not. Then she told us why she couldn't stand us. She was sick of me before she'd even met me. She hated the idea of having to work with a child and said that I'd tried to pull strings to get to camp school instead of her, which of course I hadn't, but she wouldn't listen.

My faults were mild compared with those of the others. This 'discussion' lasted for over four hours. In the end, we realised she was enjoying herself and seemed to be thriving on the argument; we were going round in circles, so put a stop to it and all went to bed.

While the argument had been going on, Johnny should have walked over to the dormitory to check the kids were settled for the night, which unfortunately didn't happen. Two of the young men at the mission managed to get into the dormitory and stayed all night. We hoped nothing had happened, but the following day the boys were sent to the police in Wyndham to tell their stories. Louisa decided to sleep in the dormitory, armed with a heavy woomera. When the launch arrived back from taking the boys to Wyndham, a constable was on board, with a very concerned-looking Bill.

One of the two young men was a bad egg as far as the mission was concerned and, after many previous misdeeds, was on his last chance to make good before being asked to leave. With a new wages scheme for Aboriginal workers imminent, Bill had been trying to get the Oombulgurri to understand that in future their work would be for money not rations, and that they could spend their money on rations at the mission or in Wyndham. But they had to accept the good and the bad of the white way of life: that included obeying the law, which was why the police had been brought in.

The girls involved were taken aside on the arrival of the constable and were not allowed to talk to anyone until they had been interviewed. The last one was interviewed at 3 p.m. and came out at 4.30. It appeared that the inevitable had happened, but we now had to wait to see what eventuated. We had our fingers crossed because the girls were only fourteen and fifteen, too young to be mothers.

The new dormitory was near completion and looked very modern in comparison to the old one. As a last-minute addition, one end of the dormitory was walled off, with a door into the dorm. This would now be Robert and Louisa's new home.

12

VISITORS

Two days after the police had been, we had an unexpected visit from three doctors and a nurse. They had been flown in to conduct TB and hookworm testing. Hookworm was rampant, especially among the kids, who would run around barefoot—and some of the younger ones didn't like using the toilets, despite prompting from adults. The arrival of the medicos caused a minor panic of bed shifting and food cooking among the staff because we had not been told of their imminent arrival. But we fitted them in somewhere.

We had the Mantoux skin test for TB, and those who were negative had the BCG vaccine two days later. We all received the hookworm treatment. We'd been taking sulphur tablets for trachoma for some time prior, at the matron's suggestion, and this had made me and several others feel very sick. The thought of treatment for hookworm was not pleasant, but of course we did it.

The doctor in Wyndham had previously sent out allergy creams and pills for my hands, but now one of the visiting doctors diagnosed my condition as cheiropompholyx (*cheiro*—hands, *pompholyx*—bubbles). It's a type of eczema similar to prickly heat and caused in almost the same way— from sweat trapped beneath the skin. It apparently occurs most in people prone to nasal allergies; I had always been prone to hay fever. The treatment was to keep my hands dry and wrapped in bandages for four or five days, instead of smothered in allergy cream. My letter writing and blackboard work became comical for a few days because of my awkward mummy-wrapped hands and fingers!

That Saturday the matron took our visitors, the dormitory girls and me in the truck to Gingarlmerri (Moon Place); we commonly called it Camera Pool, because it was so beautiful people wanted to photograph it. It was a big freshwater pool with high cliffs on either side, about eight kilometres from the mission, with stunning rock paintings on sections of the cliffs. This was where our fresh water was pumped from, when the water pump decided to work, travelling over the Jump Up and down into the mission. The trip to the pool was always via Djadjamerri (Father's Place), a high, long cliff; you could stand there and see where the salt water met the fresh.

We had a lovely picnic and swim at Gingarlmerri, though the truck didn't want to bring us home, stopping about one and a half kilometres out from the pool on the way back. Time was racing on and we had small girls aboard. Despite the dingoes coming out in the dark, I jogged eight kilometres across country to get someone to bring the tractor to tow them in. It was the most enjoyable fifty-five minutes I had spent for some time—jogging over the wild rugged north, feeling very hot, and dodging wildlife. I arrived home in record time, let

Bob know about the truck, had a dry shower with a towel (because the water pump was playing up again) and created a mock fish out of grated potatoes to welcome the twelve people who were coming back in the truck.

They arrived safely in the dark, but how they did so was nothing short of a miracle. Just before the beginning of the steep, rocky, winding track coming down from the Jump Up, the truck's brakes failed and it started to hurtle down, gathering speed and bouncing the kids, billies and visitors around in the back. By good management, with Matron at the wheel, the truck turned the corner most un-sedately at the bottom of the Jump Up, crashed through a narrow gate and coughed its way along the home straight, with its passengers and onlookers screaming. They arrived at the mission to find the water pump had started up again; it spluttered its relief and abundant water poured from it to wash away all memory of the earlier dramatic events.

The following day we had a farewell afternoon tea and church service for our medico visitors, then nearly everyone went down to see them off on the launch. Lisa went back ahead of everyone else and, when we passed the Mission House, we could see her in the office talking to Bill. We thought no more about it, and Johnny put the dormitory kids to bed before joining us to wash the medical visit down with a cup of coffee. Just as Johnny was putting the cup to her lips, Bill asked her to come to his office to defend herself against complaints made by Lisa.

About ten minutes later, our visiting nurse, whom we'd only just farewelled, suddenly appeared with a devilish mud-splattered grin and asked would we kindly pass out some towels and hide our eyes because she was leading half a dozen men, all of them dressed only in mud and underpants. The launch had become stuck in the mud as the tide had gone out and all its passengers had had to wade waist-deep across the mud back to shore, and then back to the mission.

The time was now about 10 p.m. Our visitors were in need of refreshment and would want breakfast in the morning. The bread position being low, I made some scones for supper, and for the visitors' breakfast and lunch the next day. The scones turned out like biscuits, because I had taken the flour from the bottom of a drum of home-made self-raising flour, but they weren't too bad when toasted. The visitors settled down for the night, knowing they would need to get up at 5.30 a.m., when they would make another attempt to escape on the tide.

At midnight Johnny walked back in, looking very pale and shaken. The argument had been practically a rehash of the previous one, in which we were all involved, but all the nasty coarse stabs this time were aimed at Johnny alone. Bill had been in hospital during the previous argument, but when he heard about it he felt sick. He told Lisa that the next disturbance she caused on the mission would mean that she would go. She promised to pull her head in, and she did try to do so, by keeping out of everyone's way. After all of this, Bill seemed especially out of sorts.

Later that week a discussion between Johnny, Sheila, Bob and myself, about the church and religion, came to a head. We Quakers tend not to talk about our religion with others, though I did enjoy their discussions, trying to work out ways to make religion more relevant. Matron led many interesting late-night discussions, which I found engaging and enjoyable.

However, I became worried that everyone was doing too much talking, until all hours of the morning, which meant their daily work was less effective.

Meals and general conversation suffered, as did the work of other people as they tried to pick up the slack. I was finding myself quite often having to get meals for everyone, as Johnny was too tired or still asleep. I remember thinking that while all this talk was interesting, there was the present to think of. Our work with the kids and the people I loved was what we were really there for.

13

BEING HAD

One quiet Saturday morning, Lisa was away and the dormitory girls were out with Louisa. I sat at my desk writing a letter home when an enormous willy-willy roared across the mission, straight for the hospital clothesline. I watched as three pillowslips floated up about almost a kilometre into the air like they were balloons. Blankets and sheets scattered everywhere, and later empty kero tins were found at Gingarlmerri eight kilometres away, so goodness knows where the pillowslips ended up.

Not long after this, the launch arrived carrying Constable Morrow from Wyndham. First, he had alighted further up the river and made a surprise dog raid at the camp there, where a number of dogs were shot to reduce numbers, then he came to the mission to see Bill. He asked to see Johnny, and promptly arrested her.

Our self-righteous, goody-goody, supposedly rich matron, who I thought knew everything and was generous in word at least and who I felt had really been a good friend to me, had been arrested! The charges were not against Mrs Johnson, as she called herself, but someone with another name. Johnny had no money and had written some very bouncy cheques. She had also apparently been a drug addict and been mixed up in a case of immorality in a girls' school. Above all, she was a first-rate teller of fibs.

We had all certainly been fooled in our religious discussions with her, and about her views on corporal punishment, her qualifications, her speeches about her wealth and properties in England and New Zealand. The number of times I'd been had—we had all been had—was embarrassing. Besides losing two pairs of sandals to her, I'd been writing letters to non-existent people, thanking them very kindly for offering to buy material for Guide uniforms and telling them how much we needed. Goodness knows what the people receiving these letters thought.

Through the mission, Johnny had bought a watch in Wyndham and had been promising to pay for it each mail, when she expected her wealthy father's cheque to arrive. It hadn't, of course, and never would! No one worried about immediate payment for anything at the mission, because money was such a rare commodity that it was hardly handled by the staff at all.

Bill had known the truth about her for three weeks and had been uncharacteristically niggly with everyone, due to worry. The Wyndham police had apparently been on her trail for some time.

Just after the arrest, Sheila paid the money that Matron owed the mission. Johnny hadn't paid for a thing on the mission and Sheila had paid for all her tobacco. I think that

Sheila was practically out of money, except for her one pound a week wage and her widow's pension. She had been planning on sending her daughter home to her mother's for the school holidays, but now couldn't afford it. Poor Sheila.

The matron was fired from the mission—going that day. Once more—no matron. The only thing secure about life at Forrest River seemed to be the scenery.

~

After Johnny was taken away, we had a wonderful time laughing at ourselves and the suckers we had been. Here are some of the things we were 'had' on.

- Trachoma. I'm pretty sure no one had had it because my eyes were supposed to be the worst and later the doctor in Wyndham told me that I had definitely not had it, or else he would be able to see the scars. The 'epidemic' had broken out with the arrival of the first willy-willies, when dust was blowing around, and, no doubt, talking about eyes would make people rub them, causing them to become red. Poor Sheila had gone without morning or evening meals to give out sulphur tablets and put ointment in the eyes of over seventy people.
- Johnny told Sheila and Bill, confidentially, about her ghastly war experiences while she was supposedly with the intelligence corps.
- She told us that she had written down to Perth for parcels of hospital equipment for Sheila.
- She had offered Bill six hundred pounds as an anonymous donation for play equipment for the children. We had had

a number of staff meetings, excitedly discussing how this would be spent, but we still hadn't decided before Bill woke up to her.

- Whenever there had been a discussion or something that she didn't like, she put on a migraine attack and Sheila would look after her. She always had Sheila mixing egg flips and making concoctions for her because she couldn't keep any food down, owing to stomach ulcers caused by worry about her work. Milk was a bit of a luxury that we used sparingly, but, as far as we knew, milk and egg flips were her only food intake at such times. Sheila didn't actually see or hear her bring her food up; as the matron, she had cooked the staff and dormitory meals, so she could easily have supplemented her milk diet with plenty of solids.

- As a great concession, she had told us a secret. She was going to get her son sent out from England to be with her. I was supposed to bring him back with me after the Christmas holidays, but then there was a delay. Two weeks after I agreed to bring him, his grandmother was diagnosed with cancer, but apparently they would still send him out if Johnny insisted. Of course, she didn't.

These are only some of the stories she spun. The only fact of which Bill had definite proof was that she did have a BA with Honours in Psychology. She must have used her knowledge of psychology to fool us, because she could certainly convince people of things while they were with her. To suspect her would have seemed as silly to me as to suspect, say, Kath Skipsey!

The final chapter in the matron story was when the launch got stuck on the mud as it was taking her away. Sheila insisted on accompanying her; although she realised Johnny had done something wrong, she wouldn't believe it all and wanted to help her, so she was going with her. Getting stuck in the mud was a good thing because it gave Bill the opportunity to persuade Sheila that Johnny was phony. However, when Sheila agreed to leave the launch, Johnny, or whatever her name was, jumped off the boat and ran across the deep mud to the other side. She set off across the plain, barefoot.

Bill and Sheila took no notice, but Bill sent one of the men after her. The sight of a large woman covered in mud tearing across the country chased by an Oombulgurri man with a spear must have been something.

14

SHUT DOWN

Louisa took on the duties as matron. As far as Bill was concerned, the mission would not be hiring another white matron.

As the second term came to an end, we had a wonderful school concert and then, on the Saturday after term finished, held the school's annual sports day out near the Daddaway Tree. The whole community came out and was involved, as spectators or athletes. It began at about 7.30 in the morning and, with a three-hour break in the middle of the day to avoid the worst of the heat, we finished late in the afternoon. It was such a fun day, and just what we all needed after a tumultuous few weeks. We held various track and field events as well as novelty races—wheelbarrow races, potato races and three-legged races for all ages.

Having been a bit of an athlete at school and uni, I fancied my chances in the Village Women's Championship, a seventy-five-yard (just under seventy metres) dash, my favourite event. As it turned out, it was just two yards too far for me: as I tried to catch Gwen, my legs gave way and I skidded in on my stomach, amid much laughter and '*arlees*' from the villagers. Everyone had tea on the grounds after all the events, then there was the prize giving, before going back to the mission for a Saturday night movie at the brand-new community centre, Frewer Hall.

I was staying at the mission for the holidays and kept myself busy cleaning the kitchen, and going out with Louisa and the dormitory kids for a couple of days. Most of the Oombulgurri families left the mission during school holidays, camping and hunting for days on end in their traditional ways. Unfortunately there was a nasty accident. One of Lisa's students, thirteen-year-old Ray Mitchell, nephew of my artistic friend Crispin, had his leg badly crushed by a falling rock and had to be airlifted out to Derby. He would eventually have the leg amputated and would be welcomed back after months of rehabilitation.

Around the same time that school started back, the new wages system was brought in for the Aboriginal people working on the mission, with money being paid in return for work. Bill had been having a difficult time getting people to understand the true value of money, and suddenly the card games played under boab trees by the men became a serious problem. Gambling was eroding the amount of food being purchased, and its occurrence at the mission was increasing. It wasn't just a red shirt being gambled now: the wages freely changed hands and some families were starting to go without food.

I remember being at the store one day with Bill when a bushfire started out near the aerodrome. Bill told the men hanging around the store that they should go out and fight it;

their response was, 'Are you going to pay us?' Bill was so angry. He did convince them to go out with him and fight the fire, but he simmered about their initial reaction for days.

The fighting and gambling were getting so bad, without any discipline, that Bill took the dramatic decision to close the mission down. He told everyone that it would only re-open when they decided to abide by the mission rules and not gamble. He said that if they didn't want to obey the rules they didn't want the mission, so he would give them a taste of what that would be like.

Everything was closed—water, lights, store, no killer for meat, no launch, no hospital or school. After the meeting, when Bill informed them of his decision, the men were furious and they were all going to leave. At first there were great shouts and rejoicing, especially from the kids, because it meant a bit of rare excitement. The kids thought it a great lark—no school! Later that night, the men started to attack those who 'pimped'—it had been mostly the wives who dobbed them in. Then all was quiet.

The following morning was eerie. No rising bell, though there was church for the staff and anyone who wanted to attend. Before lunch Bill interviewed all the men individually and asked whether they wanted to go or stay. All, except one man and his family, plus one single young man, decided to stay.

Bill then held another meeting and was told by the men that they would all start listening and behaving better. All the amenities and supplies at the mission started up again, with the promise of less fighting and gambling. It didn't stop altogether—the addiction of problem gambling was too strong for some of them—but peer pressure from the community towards the worst offenders helped reduce the impact.

While all of this was going on, Bill took me aside one day to tell me that we were going to have another visitor to the place. After letting me try to guess a few times, he told me that my mum was coming up for two weeks. I couldn't stand still; I was so excited. But I was also a little worried as to why she was coming, and why she had made up her mind to do this so quickly. After thinking over the last letter that I'd written home, about the matron's arrest, I thought that she must have worried that I'd gone a little queer.

However, I knew she would be bringing the Guide material and I felt she wouldn't be doing that if that was the case. She had managed to get enough material for all the Guide uniforms, and she was going to help us make them. Bill's news made me excited on so many fronts.

15

FLYING VISIT

Mum arrived at the end of October on the same launch as our new priest, Rev Gardner. She arrived in style—to the grand welcome for the new chaplain. Seeing her on the launch and then having her step ashore filled my heart to bursting point.

Mum set up a sewing room, and she and I started on the Guide uniforms. While I taught, Mum continued sewing on my hand-powered sewing machine, keeping regular work hours like all the other staff at the mission. The Guides came in and helped; those who were just learning to sew used this experience to work towards another Guide badge.

We constantly worked on their various Guide skills, and I would teach them Guide songs around our camp bonfires close to the mission, with the fire having to be stoked through the night to ward off the dingoes. I was proud of all the girls' achievements and the degree of seriousness they took towards helping others, themselves and the community at large.

Lisa decided to start a Cub pack to run alongside the Guides. She threw herself into it, seeming to enjoy it as much as the kids, and she seemed to get on better with everyone as a result. It certainly improved our relationship, as we had that type of activity in common. She was very good with those little boys and planned interesting and worthwhile activities.

Mum took a trip out to the camp outside the compound with Sheila and was surprised at the number of dogs milling around. She told me later that she was glad when Udibane, one of the camp's Elders, came to escort them through. Some of the old people with stiff or sore joints would ask the nurse to 'rub-em' with rheumatoid ointment. Mum told me about the wonderful job Sheila was doing and the look of peace on the old faces as she gently massaged their worn-out bodies.

On the Sunday Mum was there, I cared for Bill and Mary's children while they attended Holy Communion. Mum cooked barramundi, caught by the village people the previous day, for the staff breakfast. Apparently a ten-foot (three-metre) crocodile had also been caught, cooked and eaten. We did not see any evidence of it, so we couldn't verify the size, but everyone was very excited about it.

On most Sunday mornings, everyone tended to go out into the bush after church. Mum and I went out to trap the river for more fish as the tide came in. I joined the excited dormitory children for a swim in the muddy water, but Mum was quite happy to watch from the bank. That evening everyone returned in time to shower and change into their best clothes for Evensong, which, with Mum and the new reverend being there, was well attended. The children's singing was hearty. They really could belt out the praises, and I was glad Mum was there to witness it, because she looked like she really enjoyed it.

Unfortunately the truck did not go out to Camera Pool while Mum was there, and it was really too hot for her to walk the eight kilometres there and back. But one morning Sheila, her daughter Elizabeth and I got Mum out of her bed at 4 a.m. and we walked through the coolest part of the day to Djadjamerri, overlooking the river, and watched the sun rise. We arrived back very hot and dusty, in time for a shower before breakfast. I explained to Mum that *merri* means place in Oombulgurri, and *djadja* is father; Djadjamerri translates to Father's Place, named after the first Father at the mission.

I had been telling everyone in my letters home about the numerous large snakes around the mission, and Mum saw many snake tracks but she had not encountered any yet. Then, after returning home from Djadjamerri, we saw a black snake stretched across the pathway to the bathroom. We had fun trying to catch it with a hoe, but it was too quick and slithered away through the dry grass.

Another evening after church, Mum, Louisa and I took the dormitory kids for a walk and they entertained us by singing all the Guide songs they had learnt so well, with even the little ones joining in. It was one of those lovely family-type experiences that I had often enjoyed with the Oombulgurri, and I was glad that Mum was there to see how most of my life there was happy and worthwhile.

On Mum's last evening, the Guides attended a church parade in uniform. They looked bright and smart in their new navy-blue berets and pale blue dresses. Because of the heat, it had been decided that the usual style of camp uniform in pale blue was a more suitable uniform than the regulation navy blue made of heavier material with done-up collars and scarves.

By the end of Mum's rushed visit, all of the Guides looked wonderful in their new uniforms and were very proud of them. I was just as proud of them, and of my wonderful mother. I loved the mission, but I do remember crying a lot from homesickness when Mum returned to Perth without me.

16

ONE YEAR DOWN

The humidity started to build again, so thick that I felt like I was walking through thick cobwebs whenever I moved around the mission. It was overcast and windy, with plenty of thunder and lightning. Occasionally there would be a brief sharp shower of rain, our only relief as we waited for The Wet to break and the inevitable afternoon and evening rains. On those days when it didn't rain, it was oppressive.

There was unrest at school, particularly among the ten-year-old boys, who were quarrelsome in and out of school. Poor Avro was back in hospital, with his boils flaring up again and a dreadful case of gastro, and Harold was walking around with a mosquito net over his head and arms, and a can of poison spray on hand. Everyone was feeling the effects of the weather.

Into this mix we added a mission wedding. The bride and groom, Dulcie Eura and Ray Williams, were from prominent families at the mission and were 'right' for each other—they had the right skin names, according to their intricate relationship system, to marry. The preparation for the ceremony and a big feast was well underway and it was all anticipated with great excitement. When Mum was at the mission, the upcoming wedding had been the hot topic of conversation, and she had kindly sent a dress for the bride. Unfortunately it arrived only hours before the wedding, so it was set aside for the next wedding. On her wedding day Dulcie was dressed in a modern blue voile dress that Una Millard, one of the older dormitory girls, had somehow managed to find.

The Oombulgurri had had mission life and Christianity in their lives since the 1920s, and most of the adults had been brought up as Christians since they were children. Louisa was probably the strongest practising Christian, followed closely by her husband Robert, and as guardians for the dormitory kids they dutifully came regularly to church with them.

At the wedding ceremony in the sticky heat, Dulcie seemed quite bored and poor Father Gardner forgot the ring, so someone had to run over and find it in his house and bring it back. When it was all over, the bridal party and relatives dutifully stood for photographs and then the groom went off with his mates and sat outside the store, leaving the bride leaning against a boab tree. Louisa and the bride's mother had organised the feast: great hunks of meat, dry bread, cakes of various sorts and sizes, and buckets of tea, which we all tucked into to help celebrate.

~

I was starting to feel disillusioned by the mission, thinking it was doing more harm than good. To me it seemed a hideout for both Aboriginal and non-Aboriginal people, who lived off other people's generosity. I knew all of the men in the village were capable of supporting themselves and their families with jobs in Wyndham or out on the stations, but instead they let well-wishers from the metropolitan churches think they were doing something wonderful by sending things up to the mission for them.

The introduction of the wages system hadn't helped, though I learnt that I would be getting five more students the following year, from Oombulgurri parents who were already living and working in Wyndham. They would pay the mission for the kids to be housed in the dormitory and fed. Perhaps I was doing something right.

Sheila received a letter from Johnny, who we had heard on the grapevine was now working as a housemaid in a hotel in Derby after someone, we never knew who, paid her bail. Her letter was on Qantas paper and she claimed she was visiting the hotel for a while with some friends. She wrote a pretty good letter for a housemaid!

We held a fun Christmas party for the school kids at the end of term, inviting all the mothers, women and children, before packing up the school. Then I gathered together my belongings for the long trip home.

One year down.

17

CAMP SCHOOL

The Christmas holidays whizzed by, with my 21st birthday party being held almost as soon as I arrived back in Perth. As well as all my family and friends being there, I had asked Lisa to join us. I had been unsure about doing this, feeling a bit funny after our difficult year, but I was so glad she came. She and I got along perfectly at the party and she brought with her a heap of slides of the mission.

It was wonderful to put on a slide show for all the guests, giving them a chance to see and understand the mission and what it was like living up there. The colours showed up so faithfully on the slides and my younger brother Bob, who thought I exaggerated about what it was like—how big the fish were, and so many other little aspects of our life there—stopped accusing me after that.

Early in February I again made the long flight to Wyndham from Perth, and then out to the mission on the launch. The 1957 school year began and I had eight new students, including the five from Wyndham, all starting in Year One. I wasn't sure how they were all going to fit in, but they did.

The air was thick with buffel and cane grass seed and pollen. Harold and I sneezed our way around the mission. Both of us often appeared at breakfast with puffy, swollen eyes and we would have unofficial sneezing competitions, laughing as we went. The staffing at the start of 1957 was pretty much the same as when I left in December—Tenny, Harold, Bob, Sheila, the Jamisons, Father Gardner, Lisa and myself.

I was finding school so much easier than the previous year, even with the extra students. I felt that I knew so much more, that I was more experienced and confident. The new students quickly caught up to the standard of the others, but unfortunately the same tension between staff was still there, particularly between Bill and Lisa.

At the end of the previous year Bill had apparently requested that Lisa not continue. This had been denied. Lisa had found out and was upset; but she was also challenging Father Gardner's authority as well as Bill's. Mealtimes were strained and you had to be careful about whom you said what to.

Lisa and I decided to start up a monthly newsletter for the mission, with news from the school. The *Forrest River News* was up and running: two pages of news from the superintendent (Bill), general news, a Bible story from the reverend and the whole second page dedicated to news from the kids. The editor and the news committee were six of the older students, and we planned on roneoing the newsletter once a month on the spirit duplicator, with its distinctive purple ink. It was a wonderful way for the parents, the kids and the community to unite around the school and what we were doing.

Lisa typed it all up, and initially we had students help with the roneoing. But then supplies of the ink started disappearing.

After questioning those students who had had access to it, we found that some of the older brothers had coerced their younger siblings at school to steal the ink, which contained alcohol. It must have tasted awful. I remember the response from one of the kids, 'Mix it with condensed milk. It make you feel proper good, Djidja!' From then on, Lisa and I were in charge of printing.

Mary Jamison, who was pregnant with her fourth child, due in August, had been feeling unwell. With Bill away again, being treated for his diabetes, Sheila was helping her with their three boys as well as her other jobs. Poor Father Gardner was visibly cracking under the strain of faulty engines, burst water pipes, stolen watermelons, noisy people at church time, unreliable boat crews starting to turn up only when they wanted, and every other small thing that made up a day of being in charge at the mission.

Mary's condition worsened and, with Bill still away, Sheila became concerned about both her and the baby. The airstrip was too boggy for the RFDS plane to land, so the men stretchered Mary down to the launch to catch the midnight tide; Sheila was going to make the trip with her. I heard later that unloading at Wyndham was difficult because the tide was at its lowest, which meant at least fifty metres of thick mud to climb through to get to the shore.

Before she left, Sheila was worried about one of the local women, who might give birth while she was away, so she showed me all the instruments and how to use them. Needless to say, I was pleased that when Sheila returned, that baby was still unborn. Bill and Mary arrived back at the mission together, but unfortunately their baby hadn't made it.

The North West Camp School was on again. For the second year in a row, Forrest River Mission kids were going, and this time I was to be the teacher accompanying two of them. Thomas Bambra and one of the dormitory girls, Veronica Edwards, who were both twelve years old, were selected to attend. The third FRM student was already in Perth: Ray Mitchell had been in Perth for some weeks getting an artificial limb fitted to his amputated leg and he would join us at the camp.

This would leave Lisa with the entire school to run for the two weeks while we were away. I could hear her murmuring that I had pulled strings to go, but I knew that this was not the case, so I tried to smile and carry on regardless.

When we arrived at Point Peron, forty kilometres south of Perth, we found there were about ninety kids, both Aboriginal and non-Aboriginal, and most of them had never left the North West before. For two weeks they'd be doing classwork together, and visiting museums and other interesting places around the city.

Everyone particularly enjoyed exploring the nearby reef at low tide. Harry Butler, who ran the camp, was a science teacher and naturalist, and in the late 1970s he would go on to become the star of a popular ABC TV series, *In the Wild*, which documented our great country and the wonderful animals and plants in it. He was a passionate advocate for the importance of ecosystems, and obviously enjoyed explaining all this to the kids. Harry was five years older than me, and it wasn't only the kids who enjoyed being with him.

I was fascinated by what he was showing the kids; I asked plenty of questions and thoroughly enjoyed his teaching.

One night, when the kids were safely in bed, he asked if I'd like to join him out on the reef, as we'd get to see a whole lot of night dwellers at low tide. I jumped at the chance, and together we waded through knee-deep water and explored. Harry would pluck something out of the water and, with our heads together, he'd explain what it was, what it did and its place in the ecosystem. I was totally engrossed.

We began to do this night after night. On one occasion, when we were wading through the shallows, Harry suddenly yelled out, 'Stop, Sally, don't move! I mean it!' I jumped straight onto Harry's back in horror. It turned out to be a catfish—the spike on the top of its head is poisonous—but it wouldn't have attacked me and I was only in danger if I'd trodden on it.

I started looking forward to these nights of exploration. One night, before going out, I put lipstick on, which was something I'd never normally do. As we went out onto the reef, Harry took one look at me and remarked on it, pointing out that my lipstick was lopsided. We were silent until he suggested that perhaps I should spend the last couple of days at home with my parents; he felt we were getting too close.

I did go and spend some time with my parents and my baby sister, Susie, before arriving back to collect the Forrest River kids and start the long trip back. I was to see Harry another couple of times in my teaching life; one time he opened the new science block at my school in the 1980s. He was still just as passionate about maintaining ecosystems, and thankfully he never mentioned my lopsided lipstick ever again.

18

MICK

The day I returned from camp, I helped Sheila deliver a little baby girl. Sheila explained everything to me as the birth progressed, and I even listened to the baby's heart beating inside her mother, which was an awe-inspiring experience. There was a lot of moaning and hard work and it seemed to me that sitting on eggs like a chicken would be easier than giving birth.

Sandra Rose Mitchell arrived at 5.10 p.m. on 4 April, a fourth child for Crispin and his wife Leray. I remember thinking that every girl should see at least one birth before marriage, and that when I had children I wouldn't want any anaesthetic if and when my time came, because there was so much excitement I'd miss out on, even if it did look like you were banging your head against a brick wall to gain relief!

The week before we had left for camp school, another staff member had arrived at the mission. Randolph, known as 'Mick', Stow had attended Guildford Grammar School and studied at the University of Western Australia and, despite being only twenty-one, the same age as me, he had already had novels and poetry published and they had sold well. He had wanted to come out to Forrest River to experience life on an Aboriginal mission and, after many letters to the committee in Perth, he'd obtained permission on the proviso that he worked while he was here. Originally he was only going to be with us for three months but, as with all things at Forrest River, that didn't quite work out as planned.

Mick was very shy and quiet. He would sit at the table during mealtimes, not joining in the conversation, but instead lean forward with his head down, twiddling one thick-set eyebrow as we talked around him. He kept to himself at the start, and I didn't blame him.

Not long after my return from camp school, there was a plenty big *Gudija* (white man) row. Bill was getting fed up with Lisa demanding things of him and slinging off at Father Gardner, but probably his biggest annoyance was her keeping kids in for anything up to an hour over lunchtime, as well as after school and recess. We used to have a big break over the hottest part of the day—two hours forty-five minutes for lunch. Lisa's reasoning for keeping them in was that half of her senior class were behind in their work, and she kept them in to try and catch up.

One lunchtime Bill walked over to the school after the kids had been kept in for half an hour already when he got there, and he told them to go home. When Lisa objected, he informed her that, as their legal guardian, he had every right. When they came back into class that afternoon, she then proceeded to tell the kids that Brother Bill was extremely rude, and she wouldn't teach them again until every parent told her she could do what she liked. I'm sure the kids were privately cheering at the prospect of no school for the rest of the day!

That afternoon she held a parents' meeting after church, against Bill's wishes; she asked me to attend as a witness on her side and to back her up. I couldn't do the latter, so I refused.

I don't know what was said at the meeting, but I heard afterwards that there was a lot of abuse aimed at Bill and Father Gardner. I found the Forrest River Mission school journal at the state library recently; for that week Lisa had written that 'The parents met in the school on Monday night and gave their wholehearted support to anything I wished to do to help their children educationally. They accepted my complete authority over their children.' I had to admire her courage for fighting for what she thought was right, but unfortunately Lisa was disgusted with my decision to keep right out of it.

Bill sent off telegrams and reports to the committee in Perth, and Lisa refused to go to church or attend breakfast with the rest of the staff. Sometimes I felt that being in the mission was like being perched on a high-tension cable with a worn-out insulator!

~

Mick and I became friendly amid this strained atmosphere and would often go out exploring to escape. I would be armed with my trusty rifle, a camera and a quart pot, so we could boil a billy whenever we stopped. We were both quite shy, and when we went on hikes together round the mission we'd walk about ten metres apart in relative silence. Mick would also go off on his own quite often, but we had an agreement that if one of us wanted to socialise, we'd stand outside the other's accommodation and call out, to see if the other wanted company. This was similar to what would happen when you approached the old people's camp, though without the numerous dogs!

Sometimes we just wanted to be alone, but we did spend many evenings at the mission chatting over quart pots of Milo or coffee boiled on my little primus stove. Mick laughed at the various lizards, frogs and geckos I had collected and held in jars for Harry Butler, who had requested that we send him any that I and the kids could catch.

One weekend Sheila, her daughter Elizabeth, Mick and I set off at 4.45 a.m. to have breakfast at Djadjamerri, to snap the sunrise. The 180-degree view from Djadjamerri along the river was spectacular; at the meeting of the fresh and salt water, just past the mission, the water changed colour from brown to a clearer blue, and the sunrise reflected on its surface was spectacular. Sheila and Liz went home at 7.30 a.m., and Mick and I decided to walk at least as far as the nearby rock paintings. We finally returned at 4 p.m., having had nothing to eat since 6 a.m.

We had walked twenty kilometres, past the rock paintings to the other side of Gingarlmerri, up cliffs and across rivers, only stopping once to boil a billy and make grasshopper tea—the grasshoppers were everywhere and got into everything. The countryside was magnificent. We were pushing through the tall cane grass when we suddenly came out onto a lovely big pool, where there were rocks and water lilies and a big brolga looking at us, standing only about three metres away. It slowly and gracefully opened its wings a couple of times, took one or two steps and flew away, making a terrific din with its wings. It was the first time I had been out without Guides or kids, and it was a perfect day.

Another weekend, Mick and I decided to walk along the new road being made from Happy Valley Station to the mission, through the beautiful area known as Oomballi, another lovely time together. The idea of the new road was so the mission could run cattle for sale, trucking them out to Wyndham. Unfortunately the road kept getting washed away each wet season, and would eventually be abandoned as a workable road.

The Oombulgurri decided Mick and I needed to have skin names. We had to have the right skin names to go out together alone as much as we did. Mick was given Najiri and I was Ganjili. Oombulgurri matchmaking, but we were both so shy that nothing would ever happen in that way. Mick told me at one stage that he'd been badly hurt by a girl before he came up to Forrest River, but I was happy just to enjoy his company. By following our tracks, the kids used to know what we'd been doing, where we'd been and where we'd sat down together. I can still hear them saying 'Arlee Djidja, you been sit down longa Brother Mick!'

Mick gave me the nickname Sunshine Sal or just Sunshine. That was worth the effort of smiling and laughing at everything that was going on at the mission.

One trip I will always remember was just after we'd had a freakish storm that dropped an unusual amount of rain, 316 points (seventy-nine millimetres) in the normally dry season.

Water was running everywhere, and Mick and I decided to walk out to Narngi, the beautiful waterfall a few kilometres from the mission. We had a swim, and Mick lay on the lowest shelf of rock, letting the water cascade over him. I started a fire and put the billy on, watching as he climbed each of the five steps of rock shelf. He laid down on each shelf and let the water bubble down over him. He was so quiet, and yet seemed to be absorbing everything around him. Seeing the area through new eyes accentuated the beauty of the place even more for me.

Mick worked in the store helping Tenny, and there he quickly picked up the local language, especially from the old people. He seemed to be loved by all the Oombulgurri people, old and young alike, as they happily told him about themselves, the mission and the massacre. One time at the store, I called in to see Mick, and some of the older women were haggling and joking about trying to get some extra tobacco. The women started talking about bloomers when, to my horror, Mona, one of the old women from the camp who had adopted me as her granddaughter, grabbed me and lifted my skirt way up over my head to show them all my bloomers! I was so embarrassed, which made them laugh more, and I left rather promptly.

Mick helped by sometimes playing the organ at church, which I greatly appreciated, as it gave me a break. Evening singsongs would sometimes start up at night, with Mick playing the piano or his guitar in the hall. A favourite was the American folk song 'Pick a Bale of Cotton'. I can remember giggling at some of the kids later walking up the avenue of boab trees, copying Mick's long, loping gait and singing, 'Oh Lordy, pick a bale o' cotton'.

For a few weeks the communication wireless broke down and we had no contact with the outside world. But I didn't care—Mick and I would just go walkabout, taking food and going out into the bush for a while when we weren't working. We got to the stage where we could tell when one of us didn't want to be with the other and we could walk for miles in silence without it being awkward.

19

COMINGS AND GOINGS

As with all things at the mission, anything could and often did happen, and it was rarely expected. Tenny had to go to Perth for treatment for skin cancer, and Mick was happy to stay and help until his return.

The Forrest River Mission committee in faraway Perth sent up one of their members, Dr 'Major' Robertson, to check on our situation after the flurry of telegrams from Bill and Lisa about the one-day school closure. He seemed a hail-fellow-well-met type, and he kept saying we must have a happy atmosphere. He invited himself around for morning and afternoon tea, supper, actually any odd time we were free. Mick and I would cough and splutter at the way he persisted in describing people as 'silly asses', making *ass* rhyme with *glass*.

Mealtimes suddenly seemed very militaristic. Dr Robertson called Father 'The Padre' or the 'Mess President'; Harold became 'Weibye, my man'; Sheila was Mrs Hill. Whenever he called me 'Miss Gare', I replied, 'Yes, Major!', which did annoy him somewhat. But poor Mick suffered the most, with the title of 'Mickey Mouse'.

'The Major'—or Robbie, as we started calling him—was obviously observing the staff with the purpose of reporting back to the committee and he gave us almost a daily commentary on his findings. He told me that the committee would get a big shock when he told them about The Padre—how well he was fitting in, how useful he was, how happy he seemed, and how much younger he looked. I was relieved for poor Father Gardner. He then gave me a strange gift—a book on chess for me to study, so I could beat 'Miss Turner'.

One Sunday afternoon Mick, Father and I were sitting on Father's verandah. We saw Robbie call in to visit Lisa and spend nearly three hours there. We rather unfairly made catty remarks about marrying the two of them off, but we did wonder what he would report back to the committee. Of course, we did not know what was said, but Lisa packed up the next morning and went camping out in the bush for a few days, leaving me with all the school kids again.

After trying to cope with all of them for the first three days, I decided to split them up. I had the little kids from seven in the morning to 11.30 a.m., and the big kids after the lunch break, from about 2 p.m. to 4.30 p.m., with the usual lunch break from 11.30 a.m. to two in the afternoon. This worked really well: I managed to teach them something and keep them all happy. However, with church at 6.15 a.m. and p.m., and then supervising the rec hall at night until eight, I was glad when the weekend came around.

Most of the village took off camping that weekend. Sheila and her daughter went out with Louisa and the dormitory kids; Mick went off camping by himself; and Lisa was still at Camera Pool, where she'd been all week. She had come back to the mission briefly to send a radio message to the doctor: she obtained a medical certificate for another week and went straight back out to Camera Pool.

Robbie left on the launch after Sunday School, and I then breathed a sigh of relief and enjoyed having a quiet Sunday in the almost deserted village.

~

Sheila and her daughter Elizabeth were leaving, as were the Jamisons and Connie, our kindergarten teacher. Poor Sheila had had enough and was returning to Perth whenever a replacement nurse could be found. Bill and Mary were going to work at Yarrabah, a mission in North Queensland, Bill's home state, and Connie was going with them, in just under two months' time. Bob Morrow had already handed in his resignation and left.

Mick was still at Forrest River when my young sister, Susie, visited in the May school holidays. It was lovely having another family member come up and share the experience of such a remarkable place. With us on the trip into Wyndham to meet Sue's plane was a very pregnant Mary Therese, whose toddler was in the hospital with a horrible brain growth.

While waiting in the Gulf for the tide to change, one of the boat boys came up to tell me that Mary Therese thought she may be in labour as she 'felt sick'. I nearly dived overboard in fright, as I was the only person on board who had helped deliver a child. I made her comfortable, with what seemed a thousand thoughts going through my mind, such as wondering if I could cut an umbilical cord with a boiled pocketknife!

I went down below to find Bill to tell him about Mary Therese and found him at the front of the boat, trying to fix up holes as water poured in. Apparently, the launch had hit a rock on the last trip and the boys hadn't told Bill. Thankfully no baby was born on board, and Bill patched up the launch enough to get us into Wyndham. Whew!

Susie, nine years younger than me, is the baby in our family of five children. My older brother, John, was at this stage working in Indonesia as an engineer; my sister Anne was engaged to a Gippsland dairy farmer whom she had met at a Young Quaker gathering in Perth; my brother Bob was still at school. Seeing my baby sister again was wonderful, though she was pretty tired from the long trip up and the launch trip to the mission. I didn't mention the patched-up hull to her during our trip.

We had a wonderful two weeks hiking and exploring all around the mission with Mick, and then it was again sad for me to see a family member leave. The kids and Guides had really enjoyed spending time with Susie, and a favourite question in class after she left became, 'What will Susan be doing now?'

Two of my Guides, Susan (Suzy) Anderson and Josephine (Josie) Greenwood, had been chosen to attend a jamboree in Perth later in the year, and there was much excitement in the build-up to it. Some of my fears about their trip were allayed because I knew they would be staying with Susie and my parents in Darlington. We held mock meals at Guides, so they knew which cutlery to use for what, and they learnt how to ask politely if they wanted something.

This was an attempt to give them confidence. But I was also trying to get both girls to think, when they made the trip, that it was not only to learn and receive, but also to teach and give. I felt that they had so much to share with other Guides.

20

GOODBYES

The day Bill and Mary and their children left became known as Black Monday. We held an impromptu concert at school on the Friday, followed by a big 'modern' corroboree out at the camp that night, not nearly as cultural as was usual. All the kids were dancing and joining in, and the men in each dance seemed to be smoking cigarettes the entire time. One bloke was wearing long trousers, shirt and waistcoat, which I thought looked pretty incongruous with the rest of the dancers dressed for corroboree.

We held a final staff supper on the Sunday night for the Jamisons. I talked with Bill about Yarrabah and he suggested I come over and visit, and I decided then and there that I would. With the turmoil of the previous few weeks, I had contemplated resigning as a teacher and staying on to help Father Gardner with his church duties and to run Girl Guides, but the thought of who would look after my kids always kept me stuck in my indecision. I made up my mind that night to stay at the mission and keep teaching, and at the end of the year to travel through Alice Springs and across to Cairns to visit Connie and the Jamisons at their new home. Saying goodbye didn't seem nearly so bad knowing that I'd see them all again at the end of the year.

On the next launch trip into the mission after they left, we had an unexpected visit from the district superintendent from the Education Department. He caught us as we were. Thankfully, he seemed pleased with me and gave me a good report. He told me that Lisa would not be returning the following year, and that he thought me capable of being head teacher, unless a suitably qualified male teacher was found. I was delighted, but I was quickly brought back to earth by his next statement, that their preference was for a married couple to fill both posts for the following school year. I would just have to wait and see.

Mick was receiving wonderful reviews and comments in response to his latest book, *The Bystander*, which had recently been published in England. He also received fan mail from people in different countries. 'At least,' he told me, 'they send some stamps.'

'For the reply?' I asked.

'No, for Susie,' he answered with a grin.

My sister Sue collected stamps at the time, and she seemed to be the only teenage girl who didn't make Mick shy. The dorm girls got him down; they would fight over him and sigh '*Arlee*, Brother Mick' every time they saw him. For that reason, he started to hate playing the organ at church. The organist had to sit in front of the girls, who would critically watch him for any change in his facial expression or position during the whole service.

On our last weekend together, Mick and I compared notes and laughed about snippets of advice each had received from Father Gardner. Father told me not to let myself get too fond of 'Old Mick'—no doubt thinking of the three years Mick planned to work as a professor in Adelaide before a possible move to England. Then, after Mick talked to Father about what was going to happen if he went to England, Father warned him not to get married just yet, because he was too young.

Mick did mystify me somewhat and I was sad for weeks after he left, especially because I knew that Sheila would be leaving whenever a new nurse could be found. It wasn't until the following year, when Mick's book *To the Islands* was published, that I realised how much of the place and its people he had absorbed. That book won him the Miles Franklin Award and, to our great surprise, he dedicated it to Bill Jamison and me.

I would meet up with Mick a couple of times later in my life, but the time we shared at the mission, and our friendship there, could never be replicated. When he passed away in 2010, the University of Western Australia asked me to talk about our time together at the mission. I stood up and gave a talk; I showed some of the photos I had taken, and gave my impression of him telling off the old women in the store after they tried to cajole more tobacco out of him. Then I held aloft for all to see my trusty quart pot, the same one we had taken out into the bush, and which I still have.

Such great memories, of a great time together.

21

ABRACADABRA

I had been asking my parents to look into finding me a wireless for some time and was very excited when one finally arrived. It was wonderful! I pulled it out of its box, put in fresh batteries and turned it on. Whether it was simply the shock of hearing it emit sound or whether it was the volume, I don't know, but I nearly fell over when the music blared out. And that was without the aerial even being up! I fiddled with the dials and more music and voices came out. I felt like I could hear just about every station in the world; I could listen to discussions between Russians, Americans, Indonesians, Malays, Australians—and nearly every short-wave station that I could understand had something of interest on it.

With much excitement, Sheila came over that first night and we listened to a radio drama—a murder mystery. I had been dreadfully sick with a bad bout of tonsillitis and still wasn't one hundred per cent, but this simple wireless provided me with a wonderful glimpse into the outside world. Along with my Guides, that little wireless was a reason to feel good.

The mission still hadn't replaced Bill and it didn't look likely to happen any time soon. The committee had been advertising widely but there were no suitable applicants, so poor Father Gardner was acting superintendent, on top of his parish work. Then Harold handed in his resignation and was leaving. He was to be replaced by another handyman, Ken Randall, who came with his wife and young family. Harold worked with Ken for a couple of weeks to show him the ropes before leaving.

Our first anniversary of the commencement of the Guide company was coming up and I asked the girls what they'd like to do. Someone said, 'Have a fancy dress party!' It was probably someone who had been to camp school because the others didn't really know what a fancy dress party was. When it was explained to them, they all heartedly agreed and a few other additions were made—decorate the hall; play games; have folk dancing, which we'd been practising in the hall at nights; have singing and a big feed.

We dropped the big feed idea and left it at a mug of cordial and a piece of cake each. I expected to have to chase people to do the decorating and to fix up a lot of costumes, but I was surprised when everyone at the mission suddenly seemed to know about it. Usually when anything was initiated at school or Guides it was forgotten about until I brought it up again. The Oombulgurri hardly ever planned or thought ahead, but on this occasion the excitement of the kids seemed to make it all happen.

We were now up to fourteen Girl Guides—including Nita and Joy Bambra, who had Afghan heritage and were very active and agile; Sheila's daughter Elizabeth; and Lovie Ruston.

Lovie was a character, always smiling, always happy. They were all so excited. All I ended up doing was making a cake and showing them how to make a paper cone to squeeze icing through to decorate it. And I did organise the games for the evening.

The costumes were marvellous, and the whole village seemed to be involved. Mothers were busy sewing for a couple of days before; because my tonsillitis took its toll on me once again, Sheila stepped in to help. We ended up having a clown, a lion tamer, a dancing girl, a drummer and an acrobat—these five came together and formed 'The Abracadabra Circus'. There was also a tennis girl, two stockwomen, a native American girl, a Dutch girl, a ballerina, a senorita and a girl in evening dress. Lovie was authentically dressed for corroboree and Sheila came as Guy Fawkes.

The evening was supposed to be a private affair, for Guides only. I had asked everyone else to keep away but, if they must come, to look without being seen or heard. My reason for doing this was because the girls were notoriously shy, and I was worried an audience would spoil everything. I need not have worried. Every villager was there, as well as the Randalls, Father Gardner and Harold; we also had a Mr Cranswick and Mr McDonald from the mission committee, who were up assessing the cattle program, and Tenny. They all stood jammed against the walls of the hall and wouldn't go away!

All the games I'd organised became stage acts. The Guides had all been too shy to parade individually at the beginning, but as we started playing games, they soon lost their shyness completely and forgot the onlookers. When we had singing, they wanted to do all the action songs, including the

Guide camp song 'Mrs O'Grady', during which they put on airs and walked around like models, enthusiastically singing 'Mrs O'Grady was a lady'. They had never been game enough to do that even among themselves before. Although there was much screaming and fun, they were very orderly and raised their hands quickly when suggestions were needed.

I kept putting the supper off. I felt dreadful that our one cake and cordial wasn't going to feed all these people. I thought they would get bored and drift away, but they didn't. In the end, I had to address them and tell them that unfortunately we didn't have enough to share, so if they didn't want to watch us eat, they should go now.

Later, after I had said 'Goodnight' to all the Guides, they insisted on staying and cleaning up without being asked to. The two youngest recruits were still excited, and they ran up to the piano and started ping-ponging up and down the keys. I watched as one of the older girls went up to them and said, '*Arlee*, Guides, don't go silly!' while she firmly closed the piano lid. That did make me smile because, out of all the Guides, she would have been the first to be silly.

This whole occasion might seem small and not much to get excited about, but excited I was. I think my eyes must have been shining with happiness. It had been so different from the lack of enthusiasm and indifference to things in general that could so often overtake the village and the mission. It truly had been a magical night.

22

EXODUS

My workload was getting ridiculous, trying to juggle teaching and all the other duties that seemed to have been heaped on me. With Mick gone and Sheila leaving, I was learning to be both a nurse and a storekeeper, because Tenny still hadn't returned from Perth.

My nursing career began with trying to give poor Avro a shave with a less-than-sharp razor. Needless to say, I didn't succeed and Sheila had to take over. She gave me a refresher on giving needles, but I hoped the new nurse would arrive before Sheila left—for the sake of myself and any poor person to whom I would be administering them.

My Saturday mornings were spent working at the store, so I changed the Guides meetings from Saturday mornings back to Thursday nights. Then, to top it off, my tonsillitis flared up again and, after an 'over the radio' consultation, I had to give myself multiple penicillin needles.

I was feeling fed up again. Mum was sending up material to make underpants for the men and boys; we generally made the girls' underwear out of old bleached flourbags. This was keeping me busy and also some of the women, who would come in to use my hand sewing machine to make clothes for themselves. On top of that, pots and pans went missing, only to be found left at the river or squashed flat after being jumped on by kids. Mugs and china cups also disappeared, but most in the village preferred drinking straight from the billy that the tea was made in. Less washing up, I suppose, but I was feeling frazzled. The villagers seemed to be doing nothing for themselves, while a few of us looked after them. The men would go out to 'work', but when Father Gardner went out to check on them he found them playing poker under a tree.

I really questioned at the time why the mission was in the state it was and came to three conclusions. One, that there were not enough staff to teach, supervise and enforce discipline. Two, there was not enough useful, interesting work for the men. And three, prior to the white man's arrival the Oombulgurri never worried themselves over much, except getting food and water at least once a day. With us doing that for them at the mission, why should they bother with anything else?

In the middle of all this, I received a letter from Cap, telling me about the opening of a new Guide and Scout hall in Darlington; she described how so many willing workers had turned up, working in the mud and rain, for something they all believed in. The hall was opened by the Governor and Lady Gairdner, and my family had been there. Cap had seen photos of my Guides at Forrest River, and she gently reminded me why I was at the mission and why it was so important—I was a teacher.

I had been so busy that I didn't organise a trip away for the September school holidays. Sheila left, leaving another hole in my friendship group; she was to be replaced by Sister MacMillan, who would be arriving shortly.

Father Gardner was taking some well-deserved time off and I became responsible for switching off the lights and batteries at night, and Father showed me how to work the radio by myself. I spent the first week of the holidays cleaning out kitchen cupboards and going out shooting with my rifle. On my first outing, I managed to down two ducks, so it was duck for dinner. At least I wouldn't starve. Without school to keep me busy, I was quite homesick, thinking of all my family at home and me isolated on the mission. I imagined they'd be having light, carefree conversations, and for two nights in a row I dreamt that I went home without any warning and dropped into the middle of it all.

Most of the Oombulgurri were out hunting and camping. To while away the time, I started painting all the kitchen cannisters green, with red labels, and I began to think I was going mad. I went out shooting with the new handyman, Ken Randall, and two Oombulgurri. One of them shot a turkey, and then all three had a shot at another one and missed before I hit it. When we went to retrieve it, we found I'd shot it straight through the heart! 'Our women can't shoot straight,' the Oombulgurri men said, and Ken replied, as quick as anything, 'That's why Sister Gare isn't married!'

After a week I couldn't work the radio, so it had to be taken into Wyndham for repairs. Watching the launch leave, and with so few people in the mission, I felt really cut off from civilisation. The launch returned with our new nurse, mail and supplies and the news that the radio had to be sent to Darwin for repair. Nurse MacMillan was a whirlwind, a very efficient middle-aged South African who insisted everything had to be spotlessly clean. Cockroaches made her ill, and she walked around with an insect spray can, swamping me a couple of times. I thought to myself that the Wet Season was going to be interesting for her.

By the end of the second week, Tenny was back but hibernating. Sister MacMillan and Ken, his wife Marie and their two children were all keeping to themselves, and nearly all the Oombulgurri were out bush. Robert suggested I join him, Louisa and the dormitory kids for a trip out to the old massacre site, about thirty-five kilometres away, in the second week of the holidays. A five-day bush trip.

They had already left by the time I'd tidied everything up and shown Sister MacMillan how to do the lights and other caretaker duties on the Friday night. I set off to join them on the Saturday morning, carrying a very clumsy swag consisting of a blanket, one change of clothes, a towel, soap, toothbrush, comb and a little food. Thankfully, I also took my trusty hat, camera and rifle.

23

GOING BUSH

Before even getting to Djadjamerri, I'd had enough. It was hot, the sand kept getting into my sandshoes, and the swag was heavy and kept cutting into my shoulders. I had no free hand to shoo the flies out of my eyes and my camera and billy kept swinging around and banging my legs. I'd told Robert I was going, so I couldn't turn back. Smile and sing, Sally, smile and sing.

The singing helped to boost my morale, and by the time I had sung through all the songs I could think of, I could hear the kids laughing at Djila. This was another beautiful multi-layered waterfall with a pool at the bottom, though being the Dry it wouldn't be flowing as freely as it would in the Wet.

I hadn't said a word to Louisa about coming, but she told me that while she had been fishing the day before, she had a fleeting vision of me walking along the road with my swag, so she came back and told the kids to clean the place up because I was coming to see them.

I couldn't believe how dirty the kids looked—bung eyes, runny noses and flies, clouds of them. *Whatever possessed me to do this?* I thought to myself. I asked Louisa if she, like the other mission people, was scared of going to the massacre site, and her reply was, 'No. God is stronger than any bad spirit!' She told me I didn't have to worry, the spirits wouldn't hurt a white fella.

Robert took me hunting for kangaroos; we watched and shot at crocs and dug for goanna. Needless to say I only caught sunburn, but Robert caught a roo and a goanna, and I shared in skinning, cooking and eating them.

The moon was wonderful that night, but I had to put the blanket right over my head to keep the mozzies and the dust away. As soon as it started to get light, back came the flies. The kids slept in groups of four so that they could have one blanket underneath and three on top, to keep out the cold during the night.

The next morning, I went for a quick walk to try to get away from the flies, but it seemed as though nearly every tree or rock had been used for 'doin' what comes naturally'. The campsite was surrounded by tins and bones and, as the water had stopped running, the nearby pools were very shallow and mucky. Every time I went for a drink, I could almost hear the bacteria chuckling, 'Ha, ha, we'll get you now! Drink us or you will die of thirst, you fussy white man!'

After breakfast, Robert took me for 'kangaroo hunt'. As we walked along, he lit fires from one long stick that he was using like a walking stick. At one merry blaze he leant backwards over the fire—so far back that I thought he was about to commit hari kari. But no, he was just burning the flies off his back!

We came across one little pool where Robert shot at a water goanna. It sank and neither of us could find it. Robert had fun feeding tobacco to the fish to see if it would poison them. There were no immediate results to see. I left him there and went to join Louisa and the *wongalong* (children) fishing and having a *bogi* (swim) in another little pool. Great fun.

Robert came back with one little roo, which was cooked. The carcass was thrown onto the hot coals, skin and all, the skin keeping all the fat and juices in. Robert expertly flicked it over a few times and then, once it was cooked and all its hair was singed off, he pulled it out. He then stuck a sharp stick into its chest area and collected the brown juices that flowed out in a little enamel cup. I can't remember what organ was punctured, but I was given a small amount to drink. Robert told me that it was very special and was only given to Elders or special people. It tasted a bit like gravy, and I knew I was privileged to be given some of it.

That afternoon was spent swimming and watching for freshwater crocodiles—*aiwa* (nothing). There was an old bit of corrugated iron lying near the fire. The boys set this up to look like a movie screen, an incongruous mixture of cultures. They imagined that they were watching a cowboy movie, and were shouting and hooting with such vigour that I could almost imagine that movie.

At night they all slept around the fire, and Robert made me a windbreak shelter of sticks and brush to sleep against, open to the fire. That night I tossed and turned. I thought things felt a bit sticky, and in the morning I discovered that the bed sheet Louisa had given me to lie on was the sheet the kids had sat on for their evening meal of grey gritty damper, treacle and weak tea—our diet when nothing else was caught. There were now what felt like smeared blobs of sticky treacle all over my body. The water holes didn't look half as mucky that morning!

Robert took me up the top of a high cliff to look out for crocs in the pool below. We watched, whistled, made plopping noises and shot. Sometimes we shot together on the count of three, and sometimes we took it in turns. Just before we left, I noticed a great grey water goanna sunning himself on a flat rock. My rifle didn't go off and Robert missed, probably because he was laughing at the fact that I saw it and he didn't. We killed nothing except a little rock pigeon, but it was great; every time I looked at my watch, an hour seemed to have slipped by—about four all told.

We made our way back to camp and I slept under a shelter Louisa and the dormitory girls made for me—such a wonderful sleep. When I awoke, we all packed and started off for Gingarlmerri, about eight kilometres away. Once again, I thought I must have been mad, carrying howling kids on my shoulders over stony spinifex country. Robert walked in front, lighting fires as he went. I'm not sure whether the fire was to kill flies, chase kangaroos or make everyone hurry, but by the time the last stragglers got there, helping or carrying the two littlest ones, Angus and Anne, there was very little space left between the blazes.

Anne was suddenly terrified and wouldn't move. Louisa picked her up and tried to run with her but she was having difficulty, because she was carrying so much else. So I grabbed Anne and, blinded by smoke and stumbling across the rocks, I tried to calm the little girl down because 'there was nothing to be scared about'. Not half, I thought. Judging by Louisa's face when we were clear, she shared my anxiety.

We rarely carried water with us, as Robert planned to reach a freshwater billabong each day; but, after our sprint before the fire and in the heat of the afternoon, the littlies were complaining about thirst. I hoped we would reach fresh water soon.

We arrived at the billabong at Djingarlmerri (second crossing) and Louisa pointed to a small natural hole in the rock that was shaped like a crescent moon. She told me that small boys used to be dragged over this to make them tall and slim. But then she laughed and told me they had done this with their son Stanley, and it hadn't worked.

We had a little kangaroo-tail stew, some more gritty grey damper and a mug of tea for supper. That night Robert told me stories about 'long time'—about how he got his scars and the old traditional ways. They also taught me some more corroboree songs and Robert made me another big cane grass windbreak and 'bed' out of straw. My bed was the furthest from the fire; Louisa explained that, because I was white, I didn't have to worry about the bad spirits, so I didn't have to sleep as close to the fire. I stayed awake nearly all night listening to curlews and dingoes, watching the moon, trying to see a flying fox and killing mosquitoes. It was another cold, sleepless night with a heavy dew. We would be heading to Umballi, the massacre site, the following day.

24

A BEAUTIFUL AND SAD PLACE

The next morning, we started on the next eight kilometre stretch to Umballi. As we walked along, Robert suddenly stopped and turned, 'You smell 'im, Djidja?' he asked. 'Sugar Bag!' he said, heading to a hollow tree and chopping it down. Louisa came up and they exposed a native beehive.

The kids flocked around and we all got stuck into the sugary dessert. When you are tired and thirsty, a billy that contains some water, the crushed insides of a boab nut and some wild honey is manna from heaven. The girls and I passed the billy around and, with fingers cupped, each of us filled our mouths. Wonderful! I can still remember the satisfaction gained from those delicious mouthfuls.

The pool at Umballi was beautiful. Too beautiful for such a horrid event to have taken place. Back in 1926, in their search for Hay's killer, a number of massacres had occurred, in at least three locations, but Umballi was the site most of the Oombulgurri avoided. I remembered some of stories my school kids had told me: of the police chaining the men in one long line, with the women and children in another. After the men had collected firewood, they shot them all. Their bodies were burnt, and the ashes scattered.

As we approached the pool, Louisa told me that most of the mission people would not come to this place because of the spirits of the people who were killed in the early days. 'But,' she said, 'we know from church that there is a much stronger spirit from those. We are safe.'

The pool was thickly bordered with pandanus palms and packed with pretty little fish, big tasty fish, turtles, crocs and goannas. Brightly coloured birds flew everywhere. After playing around and fishing for a while, the kids decided it was time to cook damper again for lunch.

I decided to climb a tree to look out for crocs. This being my first real attempt at tree climbing, and doing it with a rifle, camera and watch, the whole tree seemed to shake with nervousness. While I was trying to decide which was the least important—the rifle, camera, watch or my skin—a bough broke and I slid gracefully and carefully to the ground, with my belongings in hot pursuit. I still don't know why everything didn't go into the water, because the tree was hanging right over it.

I was feeling weak. Louisa gave me my lunch, found me a shady tree and reminded me that this was not white fella country. I didn't tell her about the episode with the tree. I was woken by Louisa gently shaking me. 'Come away, Djidja,' she said softly. She took my arm and led me slowly away from the tree. Looking up she pointed to a large, long green snake that would have been directly over me as I slept.

After lunch Robert came up and said, 'C'mon, Djidja, we better go kill a croc.' So off he went and climbed the same tree

I had previously fallen out of, but he went twice as high as I had managed!

I clambered up and was directly underneath him. When he spotted a freshwater croc he'd motion towards it with his foot until I nodded that I could see it, then he'd tap the top of my head with his foot, and we would shoot together. It looked like we got one, as it rolled over, belly up, and sank. Robert sent some of the girls into the billabong, holding on to a log and feeling with their feet to try and find it, but it was not to be. Good play-acting, Mr Crocodile.

After a fist full of catfish and a couple of fingers full of boab nut, I decided to go off hunting by myself. It must have been the wrong time of day because, after making a three-kilometre circle around the camp, I only saw a lot of very pretty small birds, a water goanna and Robert sitting in the shade fishing while his trousers dried over a rock. The way to do your washing was either to swim in your clothes and let them dry on you, or else to take them off and wash them and then to swim or watch for crocs while they dried.

After getting back from my hunt, I found two large prawns waiting in the ashes—one for me and one for everyone else. Angus and Anne seemed to be asleep, so I lay down with them. It was then 2.15 by my trusty watch, but by 2.30 everyone had been shouted up and had rolled their swags. We left for the trek home, but the two littlies started to grizzle and had to be carried.

When we all stopped to camp at Gingarlmerri, I really had had enough of whining kids, so I excused myself and walked on ahead. I went back to the mission a different way and it was magnificent. I could see all the cliffs, hills and pools for miles around. The sun was just setting, and every pool shone like another sun. I made it to Djila as the moon was rising at about six o'clock and continued on. That time of night was gorgeous for walking. On all the surrounding hills I could see fires that showed where all the Forrest River people were chasing game and camping. I really swung along the track, oblivious of the weight of my swag, and reached home at 7.30, pleasantly tired and hungry.

On the way back, I remember feeling something in my pocket. It was my toothbrush and comb. I hadn't given them another thought! We were in and out of water so much, and eating rough food, so I forgot the need to comb my hair or clean my teeth. I thought that most of the white people I knew would probably think that was pretty bad, but I would suggest they try it!

I arrived back to see the launch stuck in the mud, and no one around to get it unstuck. There would be no mail or supplies until that was done. I shrugged my shoulders and headed to the shower block to wash.

Help! The sight of myself in the mirror was startling. I had streaks across my upper lip from where I had been wiping my nose, and my sleeve and fist were filthy from me doing this. There were black rings around my neck and arms, where perspiration and dust were mixed. All my exposed skin was a reddish-brown colour, except for white squint lines around my eyes, and my clothes were almost a fawn colour with black streaks.

After scrubbing the last of the dirt away, I felt like eating some iced pineapple and having a thick cup of cocoa, so I went into the empty kitchen. There were no tins of pineapple and I only had a mouthful of the cocoa, which tasted like dust because its tin had been so full of cockroaches and other beetles. I then decided on a hunk of bread and a cup of tea for my evening meal, but the only bread we had was uncooked and still rising in its dish; also, I had used the last little bit of milk for my cocoa. Thinking that I might have settled for a bit of Louisa's grey, gritty damper and a weak mug of tea, I went over to look in my fridge; I expected to find my last apple there, but it had gone bad. So I gave in and opened a bottle of 'lolly water' that Sheila had sent me. I thanked her heartily with every mouthful, and then went to bed.

~

I woke up very early the next morning, as hungry as a hunter and as lively as a kitten. I looked affectionately at every bruise, burn and scratch, and relived my whole holiday. The water at Djila seemed a hundred per cent pure, the gritty grey damper and the weak mug of tea seemed like a meal at the Adelphi. I had often been surprised to find flies in my eyes that I hadn't even noticed. Although we were always hungry, had burns, colds, bung eyes and walked for miles carrying heavy loads, we were happy. There was so much to do and so many other things to think of that I had totally forgotten the misery I felt back at the mission at times.

I know I had only been out for a few days, and in comparatively good weather, but I had a good taste of what it would be like to live in the Oombulgurri traditional way. I next wanted to do the same sort of thing with the old camp people and their dogs. We had only had one dog with us, which was not allowed near my blanket. How I wished for a few dogs or even a cat to keep my feet warm. I'd do it all again now, if I had the chance.

The next morning, I found Sister MacMillan exhausted and wanting to get out of the 'bloody place'. Lots of camp people had been coming in with burns, tummy aches and other minor ailments while I was away—an excuse to see her and get more tucker. She had had about four old people down every day for showers and dressings.

As she was telling me this, one of the women, Enid Smith, pregnant with her third child, came in with a pain. There was a mad scurry as Sister Mac tried in vain to light a steriliser. As far as we knew, the baby wasn't due for another six weeks, but within two hours, one of the girls helping at the hospital ran in to the nurse, who was trying to light a primus, and said, 'Somethin's coming, Sister.'

She just got there in time to deliver a little boy, seven pounds, four ounces—she worked with unscrubbed hands, no apron or anything. He came into the world with a chord twisted (twice) around his neck and needing quite a bit of care and assistance. All was well and his mother wanted to take him back out on holidays into the bush with everyone the following day. Sister MacMillan was horrified.

It had been the holiday I had needed. I'd been given what was a rare experience for a white person—a glimpse of living Oombulgurri life.

25

MOVIES

The new term started, but unfortunately it was much the same as ever with the white staff. Both Sister Mac and the Randalls were now wanting to leave, though Father managed to convince them to stay for the twelve months they had signed up for. Tenny was keeping to himself; Lisa would often go and have tea with the Randalls and Sister MacMillan, who no longer came to the communal dining room; and poor Father was feeling the pressure of running the mission on top of his other duties.

I had almost come to the end of my tether but decided to strengthen the leather a little by adding a notice on my flat door which read—'If you will smile, come in a while, if you won't, then don't.'

That month we had the usual cowboy movie, and another one called *Green Dolphin Street*. I was the projectionist. At the very point where Marguerite's sister married her lover, and her mother and father had just died, leaving her alone and heartbroken, and I was sniffling back tears, the projector belt broke. I then spent the next twenty minutes turning the reel by hand, until the end of the movie, when I turned around to see Father had come in behind me and was silently laughing at my new projector skills.

With no superintendent, there were rumours that the mission would be shut down or moved into Wyndham. I wasn't against the idea but, even though I had been at Forrest River for only eighteen months, I knew it was most important that the older people did not 'wander out of country'. They were connected spiritually to the land.

In my letters to my parents I said that I thought the younger families could be encouraged into work on missions or stations elsewhere because, as civilisation expands, a country could not keep supporting people who took and did not put any effort back in. Some would say that this is a concept from Western civilisation, and we should not force it onto other people.

In places like Forrest River, where the wildlife quickly multiplies and is plentiful, the Oombulgurri could easily stay on their Country in their natural state and enjoy life. But they no longer 'owned' that land. Even if we as Westerners thought they were miserable, they weren't, because they seemed to have a much stronger and more vital ability to take what comes, both good and bad. In desert regions it would certainly be tougher, but I couldn't see the value in just feeding and clothing for the sake of it. I saw a need for them to help themselves, not just have others do all the work for them, which it seemed we were doing, or so I felt at the time. Lack of staff and overwork was taking its toll.

At least running Guides helped me cope with my disgruntled feelings. The Guides once again thrilled me. When I asked for ideas for good turns we could do around the mission, the reply was 'grass picking'! The buffel grass, an introduced species that was considered to be very good cattle feed though in some areas today is now seen as a curse, was in seed again, and was so plentiful this seed could be sold to graziers to plant. We started a patrol competition after Thursday night's Guides through to the end of Monday night, to see who could pick the most. It was wonderful hearing them wandering around in groups, chattering and singing as they picked the seed, earning money for themselves and for the mission. I can't remember now which patrol won the competition, but seeing them working so happily together for a common cause was a highlight for me.

Lady Baden-Powell, Chief Guide to the world, was planning a tour of Australia and Papua New Guinea, starting with a big gathering in Western Australia in October. I knew that two of our girls—Suzy and Josie—would benefit from being part of the gathering with my sister Susie and the Darlington Guides. I wanted them to increase their knowledge of Australia and the world, and to realise that, through the Guides, they were doing the same things, working for the same causes and receiving the same privileges as the thousands of other girls they would meet. What inspired me most was the knowledge that those two girls would discover that they were just as good as, in fact much better than, most white Guides I knew.

I asked MMA to provide an airline concession for the two thirteen-year-old girls to go to Perth, and it was granted. Harold had donated a few pounds to help with their costs, and I planned to get them to earn a great deal for themselves. My parents were prepared to ask their friends to buy the beautiful fancywork the girls were creating, and we would pick and sell yet more buffel grass. Our Guides were even planning to knit two cardigans for the girls' trip south because, even in October, the climate could be cooler than the girls were used to.

26

MY BIG BROTHER

At school I started having a moment's silence when my little kids were being naughty and it was working in calming them down. They were slowly getting to the stage of being able to 'brush the devil off their backs'. It worked wonders, but Lisa still taught in her own way.

Our radio wireless was still out of action. A transmission part had been sent to Darwin for repairs; we could receive messages, but not send any out. I had word that my older brother, John, was coming to visit on his way back to Indonesia after being home for a holiday. He was working with the Volunteer Graduate Scheme as an aeronautical engineer with Australian Volunteers Abroad. I was very excited at the prospect of showing him around all of the beautiful sites at the mission and to catch up first hand on family news.

He arrived on the same day as the navy and army. Six navy men arrived on their own little launch to carry out some mapping of the river—and they brought with them our missing wireless part, now repaired. The four army men came by helicopter a few days later, and of course keeping the kids' heads down with all that happening was impossible.

Father asked us to keep the servicemen busy and away from the dormitory girls, but it wasn't that big a worry, as all except two were married.

The helicopter was parked right next to the school, and was a great distraction for all the students, especially when the servicemen regularly walked to and from it. None of them wore shirts, and I watched as their pale, almost transparent-looking skin steadily changed from white to varying shades of pink. They busied themselves surveying the bush and waterways; they stayed only a short time, but long enough to witness a couple of good corroborees put on for them and John.

I took John out to explore around the mission, walking to Djila and then to Camera Pool, staying a night at each. Before arriving, John didn't believe my snake stories and, as luck would have it, we only saw one while he was there. I knew his comments were all in jest, and he made me laugh every time. He didn't believe he'd see a kangaroo, but then we saw six. He didn't believe he'd see any freshwater crocs, but then we saw three in half an hour. He didn't believe he would see any rock wallabies, but we did see two just after him saying this.

On the second day he shot a pigeon; with an onion I turned it into a stew and then made damper for lunch. Later, he excelled himself and swam across Camera Pool so he could examine the structure of the rocks. He wouldn't believe that the pool was nearly two hundred yards (metres) wide, but I noticed that he came back on a log.

After visiting the pump house, we started back via the rock paintings. John had spent quite a bit of time clambering after two pigeons, so it was starting to get dark by the time we reached the paintings. He had told me he'd already seen a photo of them, and he would rather spend the time chasing pigeons; but when we came to the paintings, I couldn't move him.

He wasn't keen to leave the road to look at Djadjamerri in the gathering dark, but when he saw it in the twilight, he exclaimed, 'Why didn't you tell me it was like this? It's a mighty river. I didn't know you had anything like this tucked away, I wish I could see it in the daylight.'

The kids loved John and had a wow of a time in Frewer Hall one night when he sang and spoke Indonesian with them. He gave a geology lesson on Indonesia in school and had a go at making Indonesian kites. After his talk we managed to get some older boys to sing corroboree while the little ones danced. I had been doing a lot of urging and talking about keeping cultural activities going at school, but it took John singing in Indonesian to get them going.

When John left, I went with him as far as Wyndham. Of course the launch, as usual, became stuck in the mud, so we had to rock it in order to get on our way. Then—thrill of thrills—after passing two big saltwater man-eaters and John not seeing them, we had a glorious view of an old man croc about eight or nine feet (2.5 or three metres) long and very fat, sunning himself on the bank. As we came near, he arched his back and clambered into the water with a great splash.

I stayed overnight with John at the Wyndham pub. We sat out on the verandah talking and laughing, and I wrote letters home and waited for the evening, when the cold tap in the bathroom cooled down enough to have a shower.

We really had a good time, and all sibling teasing was done while laughing. My days with John had been the first I had had off since Mick left, except when I had been out with Robert and Louisa Roberts in the holidays. I had truly enjoyed the break.

27

THE DEBBIL DEBBIL SYMPHONY

The next Friday morning Father left on the boat for Wyndham, leaving me with instructions to sit by the wireless at 6 a.m., 10 a.m., 2 p.m. and 4 p.m.; to fill his fridge with kero; to charge the wireless batteries; and to turn the generator off at 10 p.m. I did my wireless duty after school and went to a corroboree, where a most magnificent dance, a Debbil Debbil dance, was performed. Four men took it in turns to dance with a bamboo structure, over two metres high and with wool wound around it. It was spectacular.

On Friday afternoon Tenny was off work and we thought he had strained a muscle. At church time he didn't materialise, so I went with Sister Mac to see him. From the store we could hear him screaming. The poor chap was writhing on his bed, with sweat and tears rolling down his face. When he saw us, he said that he couldn't stand it any longer and wanted a bullet. Sister Mac tried to give him intravenous morphia, but his veins had collapsed. We managed to give him a large dose of Phenobarb; he slept for a few hours and thankfully woke feeling a little more comfortable.

The staff attitude to everything seemed to be getting worse and worse, if that was at all possible. Despite my best efforts, I started to feel that perhaps it really was too much, even for a naturally happy person to take. Sister Mac was cooking for the staff, but on the Saturday, we were informed that breakfast was going to be the only meal she would make for us all weekend. She needed a break from both cooking and her nursing duties. Since a matron hadn't been employed since Johnny left, Sister Mac, who had been employed as a nurse to replace Sheila, had taken part of the matron's role and cooked for the staff, and Louisa had taken up the cooking duties for the kids.

With Tenny still ill, after breakfast I went to do the store, but there were no stores until the boat arrived at around 10 a.m. Ken Randall and I counted out the money for the pay, and then Ken gave each man what he was due while I gave out the child endowment and collected for the school lunches.

After this, the boat arrived, so all the men had to help unload. In the store, Ken opened boxes while I served. The worst part of working in the store was writing down everything that was sold, over and over again. I suddenly realised I had forgotten the 10 a.m. wireless session, but I went to the Mission House and filled Father's Ice Master blue-flame kero fridge. Then I went to my house and sat down to reply to a letter from Mick, when . . . *sssSSS BOOM!*

Louisa shouted, 'Mission House!' Sister Mac and I ran, with her shouting 'Hose!' I grabbed the hose and went around the front, where Ken shouted, 'Straight through the house!'

So through I went, but I couldn't get near the leaping flames. Ken barged straight in behind me, opened the doors, grabbed the hose and let 'er have it. People came rushing in with buckets of water and just threw them in anywhere.

The kero fridge had blown up! When I refuelled it, I had tried to pour the kero gently, but the flame still spluttered and it must have caught some of the kero in the tank. As I hadn't noticed anything, and the flame was still burning like it should, I had left.

Father kept a bottle of petrol, a bottle of kero and the drum of kero right beside the fridge, so it all added to the explosion, which had been enormous. It had lifted and buckled the roof; it had shot eggs across the room; it had thrown a shelf and china out of the kitchenette, a great sheet of asbestos out of the wall behind it and a large mirror off a dressing table, shattering it over the floor in the next room. The rafters and Weet-Bix were alight, and the smell of ammonia was overwhelming.

When it had all subsided, I said, 'I just filled it.'

Ken told me not to worry and Sister Mac told me that the navy men had told her that it should have been carbonated. I was worried, of course; it was a horrible thing to have happened and it was my fault.

But that must have been the grand finale of the Debbil Debbil Symphony, because Tenny was suddenly better and he went to church that night. Afterwards there was a magnificent corroboree with plenty of dramatic inclusions.

28

THE RETURN

Suzy and Josie were getting ready for their journey south, busily packing and sewing on buttons and threading elastic into clothes. Poor Suzy was suddenly sad, nervous about going, but we talked, and they knew it would be a great experience.

Saying goodbye at the jetty in the dark, I dropped my watch, a gift from my family; it fell through a gap in the wood. I looked for it with my torch but couldn't see it, and miserably went home to bed. The next morning, I went back and found it straight away; the band was covered in mud, but the watch lay on dry sand and was still going. I couldn't believe it.

Before the girls arrived back, I received a letter and photos from Mum, with a running commentary on everything they had done and where they had gone during the first few days they'd been away. There were also letters from both girls, saying how much they were enjoying everything. The photos were wonderful: the smile on Suzy's face was a winner and

Josie's straight back and open face showed the pride she had in herself.

The girls arrived back in early November. They had so many packages, together with fresh fruit and vegetables from Mum and Dad for us all, that it felt like Christmas. The girls looked fit and healthy, but I didn't get much out of them, and didn't expect to, until we went out in the bush.

For the next Guide camp we watched an eclipse of the moon. As we lay on our tummies with the ants under a boab tree eating boab nuts, the girls told me that my brother Bob was nice but had a terrible crewcut, my sister Susie was good fun, and that Anne wears nice clothes. They came back wearing fashionable skirts and blouses; they thought they were just it, and seemed very pleased that they knew a lot about the bigger world that the other girls didn't. They sang some of the songs they had learnt, and these were passed on quickly to the other Guides. We all sang and smiled as we sat up waiting for night to fall.

The Wet decided to break that night. The clouds threatened to block the eclipse we were looking forward to viewing, but they cleared long enough for us to see the moon's total eclipse. Then a great roaring started up, with thunder and lightning, as the clouds again obscured the night sky.

I felt a bit like Dorothy in the *Wizard of Oz* as I ran home with the girls. We were struggling against a wind laden with dust, leaves, twigs and paper. The lightning was continuous and all around us. Quite a few women and kids were screaming, and the shutters were banging as we came into the compound. I got into bed just in time to hear the rain start to pelt down.

It lasted only about twenty-five minutes, but it gave us nearly two inches (fifty millimetres) of water. It stopped as suddenly as an orchestra. The clouds cleared and all was calm, except for the happy frogs.

29

WEST TO EAST

At the end of November Lisa received a telegram from the Department of Education asking her if she would rather be an infant teacher at Lesmurdie Primary in Perth or assistant teacher at a school closer to where her mother lived. Lisa wasn't coming back. We knew that the department had been advertising for a married couple to take up the teaching posts, but I still hadn't heard if they had found anyone so didn't know what would happen about my position

A month before, I had secretly written to Mr Rourke, our regional supervisor, asking for a transfer to a primary school close to home. After Mick left, I had felt so melancholy, and one morning in church I suddenly decided that I needed to mix with young people again. If the staff had been a little younger or more lively, or if I had had a family of my own, I knew I could have stayed forever, but there was no one to talk to without getting grumbles for replies, other than poor overworked Father Gardner. There was no fun or social life for me, other than teaching the kids and being with the families on the weekends.

After I wrote that letter, I had a period when I was happy and started to think that there was really nothing wrong with the place, but I knew this really wasn't so—there were not enough staff or resources. I felt that, as a young, single person, I had done my duty and should be sensible and leave the old and frustrated to cheer themselves up after their childish squabbles.

There was so much I would miss about the mission: the excitement of mail days and the rush to write letters whenever we knew the launch was going; the incredible scenery and beauty of the bush; my garden, which produced fresh food when we needed it most; being able to go out shooting for our own meat, or going out bush when I had the time. Mainly, I would miss the kids and their parents. They had become like family to me—all the mutual love and care we shared. Of course, there were things I wasn't going to miss— like the climate and insects, for example—but I've laboured over those enough.

I received a letter from the Education Department, advising me that at the beginning of the next school year I would be starting at Greenmount State School, about twenty-five kilo- metres east of the Perth CBD, and not far from Darlington. In the same mail I also received a wonderful letter from Cap, asking if I wanted to be involved in Guides back in Darlington if I was going to be teaching back in Perth, and of course I said 'Yes'. I just hoped whoever was replacing Lisa and me at Forrest River would still run Guides and Cubs. If not, I was willing to do it via correspondence.

My departure was sort of expected; most people only did a two-year term at any outback posting. No fuss was made, other than organising a final Guides meeting and end of school term ceremonies.

I was looking forward to being with my family most of all but, before that, I had a trip to plan. Bill sent a telegram saying he'd love to see me in Cairns, and from there I would travel down to Brisbane, to catch up with Madeline Eden, a Friend who had been writing to me for the last few months wanting to know about life on a mission. She had asked me to stay with her when she knew I would be in her state. From there I would fly on to a big Friends' gathering in Adelaide in January, before heading home.

I was aiming to spend my school holidays travelling across our vast continent from west to east. Alison Gare, as I was formally christened, felt prepared; but Sally was feeling a little hesitant. Planning it all—buses, trains and accommodation—from such an isolated place, in a time when no mobile phones existed, I seriously questioned whether the Queen's Guide test was easier than getting across and around our continent.

I packed all of my heavy luggage—my sewing machine, wireless and books, plus surplus clothes—and sent them off with Lisa by ship, for my parents to pick up at Fremantle Harbour. I then looked at the contents of my two small suitcases, which would have to last me for six weeks until I reached home. It would have to do.

My departure day from FRM arrived, with the launch leaving on the 2 p.m. tide, and it was harder than I could have imagined. Everyone seemed to be at the jetty to see me off; I still have two beautiful linen tablecloths given to me as a farewell gift. One of the ladies had drawn on them and then organised for others to help her with the embroidery.

Truly precious and unique. Louisa and some of the older women took it in turns to hug, kiss and cry over me; by the time I got to Robert, my vision was blurred and my ability to speak had left me. He took his hat off, bowed as he shook my hand and kissed it while sobbing 'Goodbye.'

I no longer tried to hold back my tears and, as I turned around, there were all the Guides in their pale blue uniforms in a guard of honour down to the launch. We saluted each other with tearful Guide smiles and shook hands all along the line. At the end, one of the girls presented me with another beautiful gift, a piece of pine with a Guide trefoil surrounded by the three patrol emblems burnt into it. At our official break-up, they had already given me a cloth with the same design embroidered on it.

I had arrived at Forrest River expecting to teach Aboriginal students, to help them integrate into white society, but in turn I had been a student learning about the Oombulgurri culture and way of life. I now knew how to hunt bush tucker, to dance and sing corroboree, and had heartfelt appreciation of a truly special place.

It was a rough, wet trip into Wyndham, which was probably good as it hid my tears. I vowed that one day I would be back.

30

TRIP TO YARRABAH

The trip across the continent took me nine days from Forrest River, passing through different landscapes. The lush tropics changed to scrappy bush—with low trees dwindling away from pebbly ground to just rock and no trees, with heat mirages in the distance—before returning to tropical North Queensland.

In the middle of all this was a place that will always stick with me: Soudan Station. It sat on the Barkly Tableland, 130 kilometres from the Queensland border. From the bus, I caught sight of the homestead and six little galvanised huts on stilts for the workers. Fat cattle seemed to be thriving on the small tufts of grass among the pebbles, and as we pulled up, a mother with four little kids ran barefoot down to meet the bus. The kids had fair hair and brown faces with turned-up, freckled noses; the mum was thin and had a happy face. They all laughed as they took their Christmas mail. As they left, the littlest, a small boy of about four, waved to me by opening and shutting his fist and saying, 'Merry Christmas.' It was only then that I realised it should have been me who said that first, but I was too busy swallowing the lump in my throat as I looked at the scene unfolding in front of me. I still hoped I would find a cattleman someday.

The bus stopped at multiple towns until we reached Mt Isa where I would stay for two nights. I caught two trains on the trip from Mt Isa to Townsville, and then a change of trains onto Cairns. The overnight train trip on Christmas Eve from Townsville to Cairns was dreadful; there is no other word for it. I was heading into more trouble than any young woman would want to endure. The train was a mixed goods and passenger train, and as we sped into the night, I realised I was the only female on board with twenty-five male passengers. I was young, single and very naïve.

Perhaps it was because they were getting into the Christmas spirit, but it seemed all the men were well lubricated with alcohol by the time night fell. I wasn't drinking and settled down for the night in my allotted compartment. My first 'visitor' was a very drunk, heavily-accented Italian sugar cane farmer from Tully. He proposed to me almost instantly, telling me that if I wanted a pretty dress he would buy it for me, or anything else I wanted. I just had to get off at Tully with him and we'd marry. I politely refused, but he was very insistent, so much so that I asked the railway guard to move me, which he did, to an empty compartment, and I again tried to settle down for the night.

At every stop, while goods were being loaded and unloaded from the train, all the passengers and, I think perhaps even the railway staff, went across to the local watering hole and further lubricated their Christmas spirit.

My next visitor opened my compartment door and made himself at home and wouldn't leave when asked. As we pulled into Ingham, one of the other passengers who was getting off could hear what was happening. He spoke with the guard on the platform, who moved my visitor. I locked the door firmly behind them.

I could hear drunken men laughing, shouting and swearing out in the corridor as we sped through the night. I managed to finally fall asleep only to be woken by my compartment door being forced open. I jumped up to see one of the railwaymen. I thought something was wrong, and it certainly was as he started making unwanted drunken advances. I managed to push him back into the corridor, slammed the sliding door and locked it again. He continued to bash on the wooden door for a while and then stopped, thank goodness. I sat back down, sleep far from my mind.

To my horror, I could hear something outside the carriage. Looking out, the railway man had climbed out onto the foot-boards of the carriage and was trying to get in through the window. He pulled my hair as I leant out telling him to get back inside. I was terrified, for both me and him. I locked the window. I couldn't get any help; the person I would have thought to ask was trying to get in! I sat in the middle of the three seats, equidistance between the locked door and window, and thought about what Elizabeth Fry would do. A nineteenth century Quaker who helped prisoners and the destitute, she was serene and humble, yet self-assertive and practical, and above all, when finding herself in a difficult situation, she would stay calm and seek spiritual help. So I sat there, as calm as I could, until the railwayman gave up and left me in peace.

Things quietened down as the sky lightened to the east. I couldn't get off the train at Cairns Railway Station fast enough.

31

FAMILY AND
OLD FRIENDS

Bill met me at the railway station in Cairns on Christmas Day and I was so delighted to see his smiling face. We arrived by boat at Yarrabah, a piece of tropical North Queensland paradise. The locals fished and grew fruit on farms, the suburbs surrounding the farms spreading along the flat land hemmed in by a tall mountain range and rainforest behind. There was a rough, steep and winding track to Cairns through the mountains, but boat was the best way to get to the mission.

What a contrast Yarrabah was to Forrest River. There seemed to be plenty of staff, and it was home to about two thousand Aboriginal people and South Sea Islanders who had been brought out to work on sugar cane plantations. To me, as a young teacher, it felt like a united nation of different peoples. They farmed acres of mangoes, bananas, coconuts, pawpaw and pineapples, selling them in Cairns, as well as fresh fish and handicrafts—mats, baskets and ornaments adorned with bird feathers and coral.

Yarrabah was spread out over a large area and didn't feel like a mission at all, other than that the four churches scattered through its suburbs. Over three hundred children attended the school, with only two qualified Aboriginal teachers—Connie, who had been with us at Forrest River, was one of them. With that many students, the aim of the school was to teach the bare three Rs—no time for singing, art, music, poetry or anything else. The teachers did a great job considering the workload, with some of the kids going on to boarding school for their high school years.

Cairns was a short one-hour boat ride away and everyone at the mission could pop in and out for shopping or to go to the pictures whenever they liked. The Aboriginal homes were much nicer than the one-roomed homes at FRM, and many had mod cons like fridges, wireless radios and irons. Unlike Forrest River, nearly all the inhabitants were a mixture of nationalities—Aboriginal, Islander and white. The mission operated efficiently, and I remember thinking the Indigenous peoples could, and virtually did, run the place themselves. It had Aboriginal uniformed police and its own gaol, which was full when I was there, alcohol and gambling being the main problems. It had income from the flourishing farms and the crafts made there. Yarrabah seemed a prosperous and beautiful place to live, except for the occasional saltwater croc that would make itself at home on the beach, before having to be dispatched.

~

One of the first things I did when I returned to Perth was rejoin the 1st Darlington Guides, not that I felt that I had ever left. Cap's letters through my time at Forrest River had kept me well informed. There were so many aspects of Guides that I have always felt are good for girls, but probably one of the strongest that I certainly felt was the great sense of service and belonging. That and the idea that we live in a multicultural world, we're all a part of a bigger world. While I was away at FRM, all fundraising and other commercial efforts by the Darlington Guides had resulted in the building of the Darlington Guide and Scout Hall. Cap had sent me descriptions and photos of the official opening in her letters, so I was very pleased to finally see and be using this purpose-built hall.

After my two years away at FRM, I was keen to find some way to link with Aboriginal kids in Perth. Mum suggested I do some work with her at Allawah Grove. Mum and Dad had become involved with Allawah through their work with the Native Welfare Council. Allawah was on a reserve area near the airport and had been used by the army or the air force, I'm not sure which, during the Second World War, with huts built to accommodate soldiers during and after the war. Pressure had been put on the Department of Native Welfare to lease the land to house local Aboriginal groups who were living in poor conditions, often moving from one reserve to another with no access to facilities.

The Native Welfare Council, of which Dad was then the chair, was recognised by the government as the advisory council for Allawah, taking any issues to the minister only after going through a council meeting. As well as the roughly twenty families who lived at Allawah Grove permanently, Aboriginal people from all over the state who had to travel down to Perth for doctor's appointments could also stay. Dad still wanted Aboriginal people to integrate into society rather than assimilate, which was contrary to the government's aim, so it would be a bumpy road ahead for him at times.

After helping out and then talking with Mum, I approached the Native Welfare Council to ask if I could start a Girl Guide company at Allawah, and they agreed as long as I requested no money from the council. Mum and I then held a jumble sale to raise funds to buy material for the Guide uniforms. We earned enough to purchase material and we had plenty of left-over clothes, so Mum took her sewing machine to Allawah and began teaching the mothers to sew, while adjusting clothes to fit the kids.

Mum had also been keen to start something for the little kids at Allawah. She figured that if we could do it for white children, why couldn't we do it for Aboriginal children. So we went around all the Aboriginal mothers and asked them if they would like a play centre. They thought it was a wonderful idea.

In February 1959 the play centre opened, and not long after one of Mum's friends, Mrs Clements, started a kindergarten. Mum then started a mother's group, then a second-hand clothing shop, where she taught sewing and knitting, with the help of a lot of Quakers from Perth. I remember going out there often during that time, helping at working bees and helping Mum and Dad with all sorts of projects.

For transport, Dad had been with me when I bought a little green Ford Prefect, which we christened the Ford Defect. It conked out not long after we bought it and we found that the gearbox was full of sawdust, to mute a nasty rattle. We repaired it, and Mum started driving it around as well. It would eventually become her car and was a familiar sight around Allawah for many years.

I began working at Greenmount Primary and during school holidays I'd help Mum teach the women at Allawah to sew. I also ran the 1st Allawah Grove Guide Company. Dad and I would drive the Allawah Guides up to Darlington once a month so they could join in with the Darlington Guides as well as having their own meetings during the week. I also attended Native Welfare Council and United Nations meetings with Dad and felt even more compelled to do further work with Aboriginal people.

I became captain of the Darlington Guide Company and Kath Skipsey became district commissioner. Having worked closely with such a vital and lively person, it came as a devastating shock when she died suddenly of a cerebral haemorrhage on 6 March 1959, at forty-seven years of age. All the Scouts and Guides held meetings that were very sad for quite a while. I tried to carry on, as we knew Kath would have wished, to make good use of the foundations she had helped to lay for so many young people. She would be missed, but I will always remember her beautiful smile and support. The Guide and Scout hall in Darlington was then officially named the Kathleen Skipsey Memorial Hall.

I had been teaching at Greenmount Primary since the beginning of the 1958 school year and really enjoyed it. The children were lovely, the parents were lovely, but it seemed all too easy. The challenge and excitement of the North West was calling me back there.

32

THE PINDAN MOB

By August 1959 I applied to go back up north, anywhere, the following year. Within a couple of weeks I had a reply, saying the Education Department wanted to start a new staging school for Aboriginal kids in Port Hedland. The aim of the school was to bring twenty Aboriginal kids from the Pindan mob, who had no experience of a contemporary school, up to an academic level where they could integrate into the local school. I of course said, 'Yes'—and then found out that they wanted me to start the following term, not quite two weeks away!

The Pindan mob originally came together during the 1946 Pilbara Aboriginal strike, when hundreds of men, women and children left the various stations where they worked for rations, to strike for better conditions and wages. With the help of a white supporter, prospector Don McLeod, a co-operative was set up, with the aim of pooling everyone's work and money, sustaining cultural traditions, educating the kids and looking after the elderly. Alcohol was strictly forbidden in the camps, and traditional law and ceremonies were to be maintained. Right from the start, the strikers considered education of the kids to be a top priority.

One of the literate Aboriginal strikers, an old man by the name of Tommy Sampi, had started a bush school for the strikers' kids in 1946. If I remember rightly, he grew up on a Catholic mission near Broome and was taught by Irish or Scottish nuns, and I think he was educated to the end of standard 4 (Grade 5) and could read and write English quite well. Tommy battled on for a while with his little school but, lacking government support, it eventually folded. Tommy apparently then left the group in 1950 and went back to work as a cook at a station near Port Hedland. Since then, no government-funded schooling had been available for the kids, and most adults in the mob were illiterate.

The strike was resolved three years after it started, with better conditions and pay for Aboriginal workers, so eventually they succeeded. Though they were no longer paid in rations, their wages were still not equal to white workers. Some of the Pindan mob, like Tommy Sampi, went back to the stations and their previous jobs if they were available. Others continued on as a mob in their traditional ways in the cooperative.

The mob earnt money by selling kangaroo hides, plaited stockwhips and carved pearl shells, and by mining for various alluvial minerals—beryllium, tantalite and manganese. Soil would be dug out, collected and taken back to the camps, where it would be placed in a modified wooden coolamon, which was normally used to carry babies around. The soil would be rocked back and forth to yandy—to separate the different minerals. This rocking would go on for hours at a time to get enough ore together to be sold, with the money going back to the mob. They also built workshops at the coastal camps and made the fibreglass boats and rafts they used to collect and then carve pearl shells.

With the folding of Tommy Sampi's school, Don McLeod had the idea of having a schoolteacher travel around with the mob. I had heard about Don over the years; Dad had been corresponding with him and sharing some of Don's ideas with me. Both Dad and I agreed with Don about encouraging the Pindan mob to be self-sufficient and to work for themselves, and also that any outside help or finances should not be linked to any religion.

Dad even made time to visit both Don and Tommy when they were trying to set up the school. I respected Don's idea of having a teacher travel with the mob while they lived their traditional life and I would have loved to do it myself. Even though I was still in school at that time, the pioneering spirit in me longed to do it. However, I knew that, once I graduated as a young female teacher, the chances of the Education Department ever allowing me to travel with the Pindan mob would be slim, and at that stage I was unaware even of what they were up to. If I remember correctly, I think there were two different male teachers who went out at separate times and travelled with the mob, but these trips were apparently short lived.

The Pindan families had been scattered at different camps and stations around and to the east of Port Hedland. After a split in the cooperative in May 1959, a group led by two Indigenous men, Ernie Mitchell and Peter Coffin, broke away from the main group and brought a mob of mostly old people and children to Two Mile camp, outside of Port Hedland, with the main purpose of educating the kids. They could see the importance of being able to read and write.

Ernie had written to the Western Australian Education Department and explained the situation. They had about twenty children, aged between six and fourteen, and they wished them to go to school. The superintendent agreed to do something to help. Most of these kids hadn't had any white education, which is why it was decided that a staging school was needed to bring their literacy and numeracy up to a level where they could integrate into the Port Hedland State School (PHSS) and continue their education. My request for a posting up north seemed to arrive not long after this decision was made.

Having been asked to start the school, and with some limited knowledge of the Pindan mob, I jumped at the chance. It was unusual for a woman to run a school back then, let alone a young woman who was only twenty-three years of age. I was informed that my services would only be required for one term and that the Education Department would be sending a man up to take over at the beginning of the 1960 school year.

33

PORT HEDLAND

By 20 September I was in Port Hedland, with the staging school planned to start up on 23 September. I arrived on the Sunday afternoon to find that my hotel room booking seemed not to have materialised. A lovely MMA hostie let me rest in her room for a while before taking me out and introducing me to some of the townspeople, including the local Methodist minister and his wife, and another young MMA employee, Peter Nolan.

I attended the Methodist Sunday Service, and then went and introduced myself to the Port Hedland State School principal, Doug Murray, and his family. He was very supportive, and with not even two weeks' notice he had managed to find a space for the staging school—an old tin shed that sat not far from the Two Mile camp. He tried to warn me how rough the set-up would be; he told me that he and some of his schoolboys had cleared a space and managed to find eighteen desks, which they had arranged between the railway lines.

'Railway lines?' I queried.

Yes, it was a locomotive shed containing four sets of railway lines and, yes, trains still occasionally used the shed!

After that surprising information, Doug told me that he had also found a table and chair for me, plus a cupboard, and had nailed an old blackboard to a wall. He explained that the school supplies hadn't arrived as yet for the new set-up, and that there were no spare pads or exercise books, but he'd managed to scrounge up some butcher's paper and some greasy crayons. I thanked him; it was a start.

By the time we arrived back at the hotel, the manager said he had a room, but it was in the men's area. Unsure what that meant but needing a bed for the night, I moved my suitcases into a small room running along the side of the hotel. I had the one window open, to try to let some air into the hot room, but there were men drinking on the verandah right outside my room and it was noisy. At one stage I had a fright when an empty glass toppled from the window-sill onto my bed. I quickly put it back on the sill, in case anyone decided to climb in after it, and I tried to get back to sleep.

The following morning Mrs Murray arrived and took me to the CWA, hoping to find me a room there, but we were told that they were full up for a fortnight. It was looking like I would have to stay at the pub a little longer. Thankfully the Methodist minister had also been looking for accommodation for me and he took me around to a house owned by MMA, where a young couple lived. The husband was a mechanic with the airline and would often travel; his wife didn't like sleeping in the house alone, often inviting a friend to stay while her husband was away, and she said she would be delighted to have someone stay in their spare room.

There was a bit of uncertainty about what MMA would think of the situation. I quickly decided that, as the occupants wouldn't be making any profit and I was happy to pay MMA rent, I would send off a telegram to that effect. I promptly moved in.

The house was in an ideal location—in the middle of town, next to the Methodist church. Its bright blue shutters made it hard to miss. I had a large room with a verandah that I could sleep out on if it became too hot. I was thankful for that, as I needed a good night's sleep after my night at the pub.

I was to cook my own meals, and I borrowed linen from the minister's wife. Once again, I asked my wonderful parents to send up some linen and, if possible, fresh fruit and vegetables, which I was finding hard to source in town and was expensive when I did.

Knowing I would need some sort of transport in Port Hedland, I managed to find a motor scooter before I left Perth. I had it freighted up and it arrived not long after me. It was a little white Italian Lambretta scooter that would bounce me along the dusty back roads to and from school. Peter Nolan very kindly put fuel and oil in it when it arrived and made sure it was in working order before taking me out to the racecourse so I could practise riding it. I found it quite fun, and with a little practice thought that I would be OK.

The day before school was to start, Ernie Mitchell and Peter Coffin found me early and took me out in a jeep to meet everyone at Two Mile camp. From the main road, all that could be seen of the camp was a track leading over a ridge, but from the top of the ridge, the whole camp came into view. Rows of broken-down vehicles were the first things I remember seeing, but around the buildings and tents the ground was swept totally clean.

There was a bit of rush and scurry going on when we arrived, with the men and women shouting and children getting a last face rub with a flannel face-cloth. Very soon everyone was lined up: the girls separate from the boys and the big ones separate from the little ones. Remembering the older boys at Forrest River, who had often needed very tactful handling, I was quite worried by the sight of the many big— supposedly fourteen-year-old—boys, who looked more like fully grown men. It was evident that many of them shaved, and even those who didn't should have. Unbeknown to me, young men were known as 'boys' until they were initiated and became men. The year 1945 must have been very productive because there are about eight boys and eight girls who were all supposed to be fourteen!

Ernie first formally introduced me as 'Miss Gare, your schoolteacher, and you have to take her notice.' Then I went along the line saying hello to each one in turn and trying to hear their names. Most of them hung their heads and just muttered something, while the others giggled. The adults became quite cross with them and shouted at them, but eventually the ordeal was over for the kids, and for me.

Looking down the line, I counted thirty-seven students, quite a few more than twenty. Ernie then told me that two older women would come to school for a while just in case the kids 'didn't take my notice'. The women would also act as interpreters, as many of the kids didn't speak any English, or only a pidgin version that was spoken out on the stations. Most of the adults at the camp spoke their own language among themselves; English was very much a second language.

After discussing times with Ernie, I announced that school would start at eight o'clock in the morning. Immediately orders were given, and the older boys and girls grabbed brooms, shovels and rakes, shouldered them and marched off towards the shed, chattering and whistling. I remember Peter Coffin's wife, Biddy, clapped her hands once and turned to me and said, 'Look at them kids, they're happy!'

Peter and Ernie then took me on a guided tour of Two Mile. They both lived with their families in small, white galvanised iron houses surrounded by fences, with one or two trees and some hardy vinca (periwinkle) plants growing around them. There were other iron buildings. One was a hut labelled 'Nomads Pty Ltd'; here Don McLeod had had his headquarters. The big boys slept in another hut; here there was a very clean dining room and a kitchen with a large wood stove, plus a storehouse and two small toilets. There were quite a few tents where children or families slept, and down near the muddy water's edge, among the mangroves, was the workshop.

When we arrived at the workshop, I could see they had been working on some fibreglass rafts. Ernie explained that the men would dive from the rafts for pearl shell at low tide, which would then be carved and sold. In one tent I was fascinated by the leather plaiting being done by one old fellow.

Just as we were about to leave, I saw one man sitting in the sun sawing through a great thick railway line with a small hacksaw. 'You've got a long job there,' I said, stopping. He just grunted and continued sawing.

Ernie said, 'Good punishment, that one.' I'm not sure what the man had done, but he certainly had plenty of time to think about it.

34

THE LOCO SHED

The old railway shed was a large corrugated iron building that seemed to have been deserted for a while. The trains going between Port Hedland and Marble Bar were once held there overnight and it was now used primarily as storage space for both the Main Roads and Public Works Departments (PWD). The stores were piled along one wall, locked within a chicken-wire cage. There were giant doors at either end, more than big enough for the trains to go through. It was big, old, rusty and dirty. I hated to think what it had been like before Doug Murray and his boys had come in and tidied up.

True to Doug's word, eighteen old-fashioned desks were lined up. They were the type where the metal seat was joined to the desk to form a single unit, some for just one child and some for two. My table and chair were positioned in front and a blackboard was on the wall. I had a lot of butcher paper and greasy crayons ready to go—now to wait for the kids.

On 23 September 1959, the first day of the Port Hedland Staging School, I arrived at 7.15 in the morning to get everything ready. But when I looked out a few minutes later, there was a great mob of shouting, chattering kids swarming up over the hill. I went and waited nervously outside the great big rusty Loco Shed, our classroom. I had a head cold and a monstrous stye on my eye, and I saw this army of kids walking single file towards me.

Over the hill they came, with the two women who would act as interpreters keeping them in line. All the boys had new khaki shorts and white singlets on, and all the girls had lovely dresses and a lot of them had an Alice band around their hair. Thirty-eight kids, another having arrived from the desert that night. My first instinct was to run for my life. They looked so big and there were so many of them and I felt so small, but I held my ground. I could do this!

They couldn't speak much English; some none at all. Such a contrast to Forrest River, where everyone spoke English. I had to speak slowly, to act out everything and repeat myself several times in order to try and communicate what we were going to do. The two interpreters, the two lovely Elders who had come with them, were telling the kids to keep their heads straight. The kids were obediently doing everything they were told, though the ladies seemed to understand me even less than the kids. Every now and then one of the interpreters would jump up and give instructions to the kids, who would all immediately shoo away the flies or whatever it was they'd been ordered to do.

I began asking them to draw pictures, hoping that would give me an indication of their education level. But that didn't prove to be very accurate, as a six-year-old could draw something that looked a lot more advanced than a drawing done by an older child. I then decided to start up conversations about what was in their pictures. I would point at it and, if it was something like a tree, I would write the word 'tree' on the blackboard and they would say 'tree'.

This was how we made their own personal reading books. We stitched pages together to make a book for each student, until I could borrow a stapler from the Port Hedland State School. Each student's book filled with each new word, which they then practised reading and writing.

I gradually worked out a difference in levels between them all and separated the ability groups.

We started to develop a routine and each morning began with a cultural song and dance, a public one. I asked the kids the meaning of them, and they said the songs were just about everything going on around them, or something from the past. They took great delight in teaching me. Anyone could sing them, they told me. The boys had a bit of steel pipe and would play it like a didgeridoo. There was a boys' dance and a girls' dance. I learnt them, and still know them. The girls' dance was an emu dance, but the boys didn't know what their dance was. They weren't spiritual dances, so it was okay for anyone to do them, even me.

Each afternoon we'd finish up singing cowboy songs the kids had learnt on the stations. Some of them had mouth organs that they played. 'The Yellow Rose of Texas' was a particular favourite. It was strange to hear them singing cowboy songs when some of them couldn't understand or speak English properly. Wherever I could, I picked out words from the songs, and we would then learn to write and read them. More words for their growing reading books.

As we'd done at Forrest River when Lisa was away, I decided to run the school in two shifts, because it was easier given the numbers and the ability range. I would start with the younger kids at 7 a.m. in the morning and go to midday. The big kids would come at about half past eleven, so there would be a little bit of overlap and then I'd take the big kids on till 4.30 in the afternoon.

After our first week I sent another request to my parents in Perth. I was after hand towels, a minimum of four, plus some cotton thread, needles and linen, as well as a volleyball and net for the school. We would all wash our hands before coming into class on a single tap out on the road beside the shed, but we had nothing to dry them on. Some of the students were interested in sewing, so I thought I could start them off with some simple cross-stitching. The sports supplies were of course non-existent, being a brand new school. I'd brought up three small bouncy balls with me and the kids loved playing games with those. We played a rough form of tennis, without a net or racquets, or softball, using a stick or lump of wood to hit the ball, and they loved it. They were all so energetic, and I wanted to encourage more sport in the playground.

35

MAKING DO

We didn't have much. Just a big space, which ended up being perfect, plus some old desks that had to be shared, and paper, crayons and pencils. Perhaps my biggest lesson from this time was that facilities are not the all-important factor in creating a great learning experience. It is more important to be innovative and to build on what is there. This was a significant lesson for me and I continued to use this idea, of working with less to make more, for the rest of my life.

We started a garden alongside the shed, watering it from the one little tap, and our first school excursion was following the railway lines to the Port Hedland jetty, where we watched cattle being put onto the big ships. We came back to the shed and drew, talked and described in English what we'd seen.

My trusty wireless from Forrest River had travelled up with me and, after putting new batteries into it, I rigged it up at the school. The students sat so still and attentive, and their eyes nearly popped out of their heads when they heard animal noises coming out of the radio. The little kids were agog, listening to the story of the Little Red Engine on ABC Radio's 'Kindergarten of the Air' program. It did make me smile to myself. There we were: me with my class of Aboriginal children not long out of desert camps, sitting in an old locomotive shed listening to the Little Red Engine over the airwaves.

I taught by demonstration, and asked them to do the same, such as putting a crayon on the table and saying slowly and clearly, 'I am putting the crayon on the table', encouraging and gently correcting grammar as we went. I could do so much practical work to help them learn, and that's what I just loved. When the tide was out, we'd go over the cliff and pick up a whole pile of different shellfish and come back and grade them according to size, colour, shape. We would then talk about them, put them in rows and count to ten, and then light a fire, cook them up and eat them for morning tea. Then they'd draw pictures about the collection, sorting and cooking of the shellfish, and we'd start to write words about it. I tried to make everything have a meaning for them.

A freight train would come from the port and bring out goods from the ships to be stored in the shed. When it came in on a school day, we would shift my desk one way and the kids' desks back the other way, and we'd stand watching as the train slowly split our class. We would watch the driver and workers unload the stores, lock the mesh gate and climb back on, before the engine would roar back to life and slowly make its way back to the port. It was always an exciting disruption, the kids chattering away as we put our desks back in place. For maths, we would note the amount of time taken for the unloading, and then we would talk about and write an account of the whole experience.

I loved making all the teaching aids. I had strings with bells and shells on them for counting frames and we'd hang them on the wall of the shed. We'd play finger games—'Where is tall man? Where is short man?'—and use marbles for sorting and counting. For learning the letters, we'd all write them in the air. I made up little rhymes for them, like 'Start at the top, come round and stop' for an 'o'. Or 'Start at the top, come down and stop, then add a little hat' for the letter 't'. Anything to help them learn.

I would ask anyone in town who had a craft or a skill to come to the school to teach, especially to the older kids, whom I knew would probably not go on to the state school because of their age. We had a carpenter, who helped us turn old pine packing cases into tables and chairs; a mechanic, who came out and showed the big boys how to service cars; a barber, who came and taught the older kids how to cut hair; and the Aboriginal men came in and taught stockwhip plaiting and the carving of pearl shells and cuttlefish.

There was no water inside the shed, so we carted it over from a single tap on the road, using two small waterbags and a bucket. People in town seemed keen to help the school and we were offered washbasins, but when I went to collect them, I became annoyed because one person said they had one but then found they didn't; and the other was a husband who had offered one of theirs, but his wife wouldn't let us use it. I was then on the lookout for a four-gallon drum I could cut in half to make two washbasins.

The free milk scheme for schools was happening at this time and we, like many outback schools, were supplied with tins of Ideal milk. After we had mixed a third of the Ideal unsweetened condensed milk to two-thirds of water, we had all these little tins left over. A man from town came out and showed us how to solder, and we soldered little handles onto the sides of the tins to make mugs, as we didn't have enough cups or mugs to start with. With the big powdered-milk tins, we squeezed a pourer on one end and soldered handles on to the edge to make jugs. We could then write about them and measure from them—there were all sorts of school subjects we could do, if I put my mind to it.

We played shops, counting out pretend shillings and pence; we talked about movies the kids had seen at the local outdoor picture theatre—whatever was happening in their lives at the camp, I could convert it all into lessons.

After spending the first week with many of the bigger kids sitting on the floor, more desks arrived from Marble Bar and Derby—in fact, so many that there was a stack of unused ones at the end of the shed. Equipment came up from the Education Department and, after starting with so little, we were suddenly flush with supplies. We were sent 'Bush Books', which were reading books created specifically for Aboriginal kids by the Northern Territory Education Department. Most of the stories in them were about adventures had by various native animals; the older boys, in particular, were using them and advancing quickly.

However, it became tricky with some subjects, like history. I'd talk about such and such an explorer going out into the Australian bush with one or two Aboriginal trackers and the kids would then want to know the names of the trackers. Often they weren't even recorded, so we made up names for them. They needed history that they could relate to; I had found the same thing at Forrest River.

36

BETWEEN THE RAILWAY LINES

As at Forrest River, each weekend the camp parents and Elders would take most of the mob out bush or up along the coast for the weekend. This way the kids learnt from the Elders and kept in touch with their culture. On the first weekend that I was asked to join them, I sat up the front in the Pindan truck with Ernie. In the back there were five or six kids sitting down each side and more adults seated in the middle.

The kids had been brought up in the bush and been in Pindan mob camps their entire life. Some of the kids said their dad owned them, as in skin relation ownership, some said their mum did. It really depended on who was in the camp or which family group they were staying with in the camp. Those without parents at the camp were entrusted to Ernie or Peter to get an education. It took some working out, because their idea of family was very different to my traditional white upbringing.

That first time we went out we shot a kangaroo and, unlike the Forrest River mob, they skinned it so they could treat the skin and then sell it. The kangaroo was a commodity for them, not just something to eat. I learnt how to get the skin off in one piece and then I helped with the cooking of the roo and I made damper. Later I would be invited out on day trips to go fishing along the coast. I loved it. I'd always liked camping since Girl Guides, but I was fascinated to watch and listen as the Elders explained to both me and the kids those parts of their land and the animals that held special significance for them. I loved to be asked along.

These weekend trips were terrific. We'd feast on kangaroo, fish and damper, all cooked in the ashes, and always washed down with a pannikin of black tea. Back at school, we would talk about what we did, what we had seen and heard, the stories we'd been told; we drew pictures, retold stories and spelt out words. Some of the older kids were steaming ahead with their reading in the Bush Books and were able to capture these adventures in their diaries, with short recaps below their pictures, a pleasure for them and for me to see. The Pindan kids weren't as affectionate as the Forrest River kids. They were certainly shyer, initially at least, but they were a lot keener to learn.

I received a letter from Claremont Practice School, a primary school attached to the Claremont Teachers' College, saying it wanted to support the staging school. I also had a letter from the home science correspondence teacher at the teachers' college, telling me that dressmaking equipment was on the way by air and that she had had a great deal of pleasure in choosing the different materials. I knew the girls at the camp would love this, but I seriously began to wonder how I could handle all of my program. For most of the kids doing the correspondence courses, I had to monitor just about every step along the way, because they couldn't read enough at that stage. But manage we did.

The practice school also sent up a giant No. 4 Metters stove—a wood stove with two ovens—together with the home economics class notes. We started cleaning the school ourselves, rather than employing a cleaner, and used the three pounds we thus saved to buy ingredients in town, and I started to teach cooking. That again was a terrific practical teaching aid for our other lessons. We measured and weighed ingredients, and we cooked and cleaned—more life skills. You can learn all core subjects through practical things if you use your imagination.

One morning we made a whole heap of little cakes and left them out to cool while we had a lunchbreak, but when we came back, most of them were gone! I lined the kids up and asked them one at a time whether anyone had had a cake. One by one, they all hung their heads and didn't answer, until I got down to the littlies. One little boy looked at me very earnestly and said, 'Yes, I had one, and him taste good!' I tried not to laugh, but the others giggled. I went back and asked them all again, and this time they all admitted to having had one. The kids had loosened up since our first week, and we usually all went home laughing.

Some of the camp adults also wanted to learn to read, so I took a dim gas lamp down to the shed at night and started to teach reading, and sewing to the women who were keen. It was lovely having the older people wanting to learn too. As well as showing that they liked what was happening with the kids, it was also a good inspiration for the kids.

On our first night, one man wouldn't sit down; he kept pacing outside the doors and I couldn't quite work out what was going on. It turned out his mother-in-law was sitting in the front row and he wasn't allowed to look at her, or be close to her. Easy! I moved her from the front of the class to the back row and he slunk in, making sure not to make eye contact with her.

I ran the adult class just as I did with the kids. On the first night I asked them their names, wrote them on the board and then asked them to copy them onto paper. This would be the start of their copybook. As with the kids, we also played shops, counting out pounds, shilling and pence and working out change with simple addition and subtraction. We worked through the alphabet, using the Bush Books to practise reading and writing.

At another evening class, one old grey-haired, dim-eyed bloke was having trouble. He was standing looking all around his desk and I thought he must have been looking for a pencil that had dropped to the floor. It wasn't until I heard great screams of laughter behind me and turned to see people rushing towards him that I saw he had sat on the desk with his feet on the seat board. The others, helpless with laughter, were trying to turn him around and sit him facing properly. For the rest of the night, the dear old chap was all stirred up and nervy; he tried so hard, holding his pencil like a chisel, concentrating with his head well down. He kept looking up at me for approval after every effort, but I'm sure he couldn't see the blackboard, even from his seat up the front.

I found that I had to write both English and Aboriginal words for everything, as they were quite resolute about words like goanna—that it was *bungarra*, not goanna—but it all worked out in the end, and I learnt some of their language as a result. It was really something watching them grasp letters and words, guiding the shaking hands of the old people as they wrote and seeing their delight as they began to recognise their own name and words in the Bush Books. I remember one old fellow learnt to recognise and read the word for emu from the Bush Book. He ran his finger along each sentence until he came to the word and called out *himayou* (emu), looking up at me with face beaming. The delight you obtain when a child recognises and reads a word was just as strong for me with the adults.

Forty hand towels arrived from Mum and Dad, enough for each child. We put up a hook on which to hang a towel with the student's name above it; we also sewed some little bags for combs and toothbrushes and they also hung on each hook. I brought in a big mirror with questions written around it, such as 'Is it a happy picture?', 'Are my eyes clean?', 'Have I washed my face?', 'Have I done my hair? Cleaned my teeth?' I had made and used that same mirror at Greenmount and brought it up with me. The kids would look in the mirror and read the questions out loud. They loved it as much as the Greenmount kids had. Washing of hands and cleaning teeth properly were emphasised and encouraged on a daily basis.

One of the older schoolgirls, Daisy Tinker, whose bush name was Djilila, was married and heavily pregnant, so the boys made her a crib out of packing cases and the girls sewed the calico to go in between the crossbars. The women started making clothes at the night school classes as well. With the school superintendent coming up at the end of the school year, we were making smart new white blouses for the girls to wear.

After a few weeks, the two camp ladies who had been supervising stopped accompanying the kids. I never had a problem with attendance; the kids wanted to be at the school, and were mostly well behaved. Not long after the ladies stopped coming, to my surprise the older boys, who had always seemed to reek of tobacco, began spitting chewing tobacco on the floor. I didn't even know they had it. I had previously seen the old women checking behind the kids' ears every morning, but I hadn't questioned them and that was where the boys kept their tobacco. I did manage to get them to spit it on the sand in between the railway tracks, rather than just anywhere on the floor, but it didn't go on for long, only about a week, as they knew I didn't like it.

The kids had begun to relax around me more and more, and started behaving like most school kids, scribbling more on the walls, giving me some backchat and trying to get out of as much work as possible. I remember sitting back one morning at tea break and watching two girls wash up the milk tin mugs, while a couple of boys were playing the didgeridoo at various pitches on pipes of different thickness that had been lying around the shed. Someone else was playing 'Red River Valley' and 'Camptown Races' on a mouth organ, and the rest were outside screeching, laughing and yelling while hitting a tennis ball around with sticks, the staging school version of tennis. It was such a thrill to see them all so content and happy.

37

SEGREGATION

Just three weeks into that first term, I received a notification from my superintendent, Steve Wallace in Perth, that the department had received a letter from concerned Port Hedland parents at the state school. There was still quite a bit of disharmony between the Aboriginal and non-Aboriginal people in the town and the district as a hangover from the Pindan strikes. Six PHSS parents had told Steve that they didn't want the Two Mile kids joining their school for fear that they would 'drag down' their kids.

I had to write reports to Steve on a regular basis, explaining what we were doing, where the students were up to, and sending examples of their work. I sent him a reply and asked that, when I was replaced at the staging school by a male teacher the following school year as planned, I be allowed to teach the Year 1s at Port Hedland. I was determined that my kids should get the best chance possible, and they wouldn't be a drag on anybody.

Peter Coffin arrived the next day with three more students—two boys aged about ten or eleven, and a girl of about thirteen. I asked him if there were any more in the bush and he replied that they were a bit hard to make in a hurry! The more the merrier as far as I was concerned.

That Friday night I was asked out to Two Mile for a corroboree—an all-kids one led by the camp father, a man called Jimmy Mitchell. I joined in one of the dances and concluded the night by singing and dancing a Wyndham song in typical white-person style. They all whistled, shouted and clapped, and the night ended, but I felt self-conscious—it felt like I'd had the last say, and I wished I hadn't done that.

Daisy Bindi, a Pindan Elder and strike leader I had met out at Two Mile, had had to fly to Perth the previous week for medical treatment. She was diabetic and had circulation issues with her legs. Daisy was highly respected in the Pindan mob, and the kids did whatever she told them to do, as they did with all the Elders. I heard a rumour from the mob that Daisy might be flying back on the weekend, so I just rode out to the drome, not knowing if or when a plane was due, but more for fun and as practice on my scooter.

As I pulled in at the drome, so did a plane. Many passengers, together with the two pilots and a hostess, got off. As there didn't appear to be anyone else, I turned to go, but then I noticed a pair of black legs in bobby socks hobbling down the steps, assisted by a second hostess. Regardless of onlookers, I ran across the tarmac and gave Daisy a big hug.

She was obviously thrilled; she screeched and laughed. Naturally she was annoyed that none of her mob had come to meet her; they were having a meeting. She had been quite airsick and informed me that she had not eaten anything, but she still seemed quite chirpy. I helped her up to the Two Mile and the kids made quite a bit of a fuss over her when we arrived, so I left her happy.

I was taking plenty of pictures, which I'd send down to Perth to be developed as slides. I had fun nights showing the kids and the Pindan mob photos of themselves. One time Kodak had a mix-up and, instead of me getting a box full of photos of my school kids and the mob at Two Mile, I got a box of slides of white grandmas sipping tea on the lawn and little girls holding flowers. I sent them back straight away and the other person must have done the same thing, because I received a very apologetic letter with my correct slides and replacement postage stamps. I would have loved to see the faces of the other people when they looked at my slides.

In town I had joined the tennis club and was often asked to people's homes for meals. I attended church services, alternating between the Methodist and Anglican churches. As soon as I arrived, each minister had invited me to afternoon tea, shut the door and asked me to teach their Sunday School. I actually managed to say 'No'! I was, however, helping Peter Nolan run Cubs. Cubs and Scouts were both popular in the town, but not many girls were interested in starting up Guides, which was probably a good thing at that stage as I had so much to do with both the staging and night schools.

We had an Italian migrant at the night school; he had been living in Port Hedland for eight years and was known to be a bit of a loner. I'd seen him at the pictures, as he would always come early, but he would stand outside until the audience had finished singing 'God Save the Queen', which always happened before the show started. He told me that he thought the English language crazy, and that all Australians, except me, were against Italians.

I thought he would have been a bit of a misfit anywhere, because of his scruffy beard, his shy demeanour and his rather pig-headed attitude. His spoken English was sufficient for his work at the Public Works Department as a carpenter and he would also carry out work around town for the locals. He was working one day at the home of one of my tennis friends when I called around after school and I started chatting with him. My friend asked him to join us for afternoon tea as a matter of course, which he happily accepted. To our surprise, he told us that it was the first time he had been inside an Australian's home to socialise!

One Sunday morning sticks in my mind. I decided to try my hand at fishing off the jetty with some of my boys—me, a thin white girl whose skin contrasted completely with the skin of my students. I thought I recognised a white man on the jetty, and by the look on his face he knew who I was. He glanced at my companions and didn't speak to me. Being a small town, most white people knew who I was and I supposed they knew all about me before I arrived, so I felt at a distinct disadvantage when I wasn't sure if I recognised people or not.

I was enjoying dividing my time between the school and the town. I decided to get a second job to earn more money for school supplies—material for sewing and ingredients for cooking. I became the usherette on Wednesday and Saturday nights at Sun Pictures, the outdoor movie theatre owned by Mr and Mrs Glass.

One of the most disheartening aspects of my second job was that there was racially segregated seating at the theatre.

In the middle of the theatre were cane chairs with cushions for the white adults, who also had deckchairs to the left of the screen. The white kids sat on deckchairs or bench seats in front, while there were deckchairs immediately behind the 'whites only' area allocated to Japanese and Chinese people. Others—such as the Malay and Filipino lugger crews, and Aboriginal people—had to enter via a separate door manned by Mrs Glass on the right-hand side of the theatre. They sat on stadium-type benches at the back of the theatre.

I'd see the Two Mile kids come into town. When they went to the movies, they would walk in with their heads down and slink over to a bench. On my first day back at school after seeing this, I asked the kids to practise walking straight, with their heads held high, and to practise saying, 'Hello, Mrs Glass' loudly and clearly and with a smile, so when they entered the theatre, they could do it with confidence. The difference was incredible; it was so lovely to see them put it into practice, and Mrs Glass was surprised and delighted, telling me later how pleased she was with them and their behaviour. They may still have had separate, hard benches to sit on, but I felt it was a very small win.

I hadn't realised why it had been so hard to teach them to look up proudly and say hello until I learnt that for Aboriginal people it was not respectful to look someone in the eye. This was why they had their heads down, unlike whites. Since then, many people have tried to teach Aboriginal people to look up, especially when they are in court, as they need to look the judge or magistrate in the eye, and to sound confident in what they say. Unfortunately, not to do so makes you look guilty. So there are different little cultural things that we all have to recognise, heed and respect, on both sides.

There was a bit of anti-Aboriginal feeling in the region because a lot of the white people were connected with the station owners who had suffered during the strike from a lack of staff. I also heard stories of the Pindan killing their livestock for food during the strike. There was also a noticeable difference between the treatment of different groups of Aboriginal people in town. A lot of Aboriginal people with mixed heritage lived in houses, while others lived mostly at the camp. Aboriginal people with mixed heritage in the town had 'good' jobs, and some were even respected in the town. It's a great pity that skin colour can blind some people as to another's worth.

At Forrest River, problems with white staff had made my work difficult at times; in Port Hedland, it was the discrimination by some of the white people in town that was impacting on me and my kids, sometimes subtly, sometimes not. This made me even more determined to help my kids integrate.

38

WINGS

One lunchtime I was inside the school writing a letter to my parents when one of the boys came back earlier than the others. He didn't know I was there, and stood in front of the mirror pulling the most hideous faces and twisting around. When he finally spat at his reflection through his teeth, I laughed and then asked him to clean the mirror.

The two of us stood at the door watching one of the other boys climb into an old truck body sitting near the shed, pretending he was driving it. He bounced up and down and moved the wheel and gears while making all sorts of machinery sounds. He got out, kicked the side, swore (I think) and climbed back in again. We laughed, but he just turned and waved. When I yelled out 'Where are you going?', he replied, 'Oh, two hundred miles away, past Marble Bar.' So I climbed in, and went too. I had always wanted to see Marble Bar!

The Anglican minister asked me if he could go out to the staging school and teach the kids some scripture. I in turn asked Peter Coffin, who agreed, as long as the minister didn't

The mission signpost just before the jetty with the mission boat moored in the background.

A view of the mission from the 'Jump Up'. The old houses are in the foreground and the church is extreme right.

The old people's camp outside the mission compound.

The large
boab tree at
'Daddaway'.

The cross on
the 'Jump Up'
commemorating
those who were
killed during
the massacre in
June 1926. The
pipe for fresh
water from
Camera Pool to
the mission is
on the left.

A typical old
mudbrick
house showing
chooks and the
garden.

A corroboree dance about bombs being dropped on ships during the Second World War. The intricate frames were made out of wood and wool.

The first 'payday' in 1957.

Popular stock work, breaking in wild horses at the stockyards.

The flying doctor taking Ray to hospital after he crushed his leg while climbing a rocky hill.

The Girl Guide company in their new uniforms proudly giving the three-fold promise.

The kids loved lining up and marching. Here they're going past the hospital.

Left: Two Forrest River boys playing the didgeridoo for Sir Bernard Heinz at the Capital Theatre in the late 1950s. *Right:* A student drawing done after the holidays.

Holding the baby named after my dad. They joked he was my 'Dardy'.

Being introduced
to my students
at the Two
Mile Camp,
September 1959.

The loco shed,
the location
of the staging
school.

Inside the shed,
the class all
together.

The older class.
Main Road
Department and
Public Works
Department
supplies are
stacked behind us.

A practical type
of teaching—
literacy, maths
and cooking.
This is our
collection from
the reef after the
tide had gone out.

'Here we go
around the boab
tree on a hot and
dusty morning.'

A drawing done at school on the Monday after the *Bukli* meeting.

The reward for good work. Tommy Gardner and Doris Mitchell on the back of my scooter in 1959. She is now Doris Eaton, a respected elder in Port Hedland and a mother, grandmother and great grandmother.

try to convert them. It turned out to be one of the funniest mixing of cultures I'd seen in a long while.

The minister spoke earnestly about this wonderful man called Jesus Christ. He then said to the kids, 'What was his name?' The kids answered 'Jesus Christ' and then started giggling. Their giggling became helpless when he asked them to 'say it again'. You can imagine in what context the kids had heard that name on the stations and in other workplaces where they had mixed with whites. As far as the kids were concerned, those two words were swear words. I had to explain to the poor man afterwards, but he didn't mind.

In mid-November the kids and I went to the Port Hedland State School, of which the staging school was officially a part, for the annual parents' day. Bishop Frewer, whom I'd met so many times at Forrest River, was in town for a few days and had called out to visit me. When he heard about the parents' day, he decided to come along as well. It was lovely spending time with the dear old gentleman again and showing him what we had been up to at the school. Not having my own parents with me, it was wonderful to be able to show someone from my immediate past all the work we had being doing, and the great results.

On display we had some artwork, two class projects, leather plaiting and pages of schoolwork. All the children took part in singing and/or dancing a corroboree—complete with paint and didgeridoo. So many white people in town told me afterwards that we stole the show. Some of the parents with whom I had become very good friends had previously told me that they didn't like the idea of having my little ones mixing with theirs at the main school the following year. However, after that parents' day, thankfully many of them changed their ideas. But not all, of course.

My seven oldest boys, who were all well over fourteen years of age, were told that they would have to leave at the end of the year, and all of them decided they would go pearling. Until that happened, they would attend the adult classes in the evenings. That brought me back down to thirty-four students on the roll and so my workload became easier, although I did miss the leadership and the language ability of the big boys.

At the end of the 1959 school year, Steve Wallace came up from Perth to see what we were doing. He seemed impressed with the school and the kids' work. He also told me that there was talk of the government building an extra classroom as part of the state school up on the hill at Two Mile because, with the shortage of classrooms, one of their classes was currently having to be held in the town hall. With the Pindan kids joining, there would be further need for another class-room. It was a logical step for us ultimately to move from our shed into this new classroom, and I was excited for my kids.

I then took a deep breath and asked him straight out whether I could be kept on at the staging school for the following year, rather than be replaced by a male teacher. He looked at me wide eyed and almost shouted, 'Yes! Will you?' He told me that he was thrilled with what he had seen.

I was absolutely delighted; I was going to run the staging school for another year. I think I could have flown home for the Christmas holidays under my own steam—I was so euphoric, I felt like I had wings!

39

NEW YEAR

The new year started after a lovely Christmas break with my family, and I arrived back in Port Hedland in early February 1960 ready for the next school year. It was again hot and humid, so different from Perth's dry summer heat.

I moved in with Jack and Joy Glass, who ran the outdoor picture theatre where I was working. Jack also worked in town for the stock and station agent, Elders. I really enjoyed their company and didn't feel like I was intruding. As accommodating as the previous young couple had been, it could be awkward when they wanted time alone. Joy Glass also cooked my meals, a wonderful luxury.

Before term started, I signed up to play basketball and tennis, and the Scout and Cub committee approached me to help with the Cub pack. My week was again full. I had school Monday to Friday from 8 a.m. until 4.30 p.m.; then I had Cubs from seven to nine on Monday nights; basketball practice from six until seven on Tuesdays and Thursdays; adult literacy class on Tuesday nights from 7.30 p.m. until nine; basketball matches on Friday night; tennis matches on Saturday; the pictures from 7.30 p.m. until eleven on Wednesday and Saturday nights; and alternate church services on Sundays, with an occasional turn at playing the organ. I was very glad that Joy would be cooking for me; I could sometimes even sneak in an afternoon sleep during the hottest part of the day.

When I arrived at the Loco Shed before school started that year, I was disappointed. It was in a dreadful mess. For some reason one of the large double doors had been removed and rain had come inside during the Wet summer storms. Some people had also been camping inside and left all their rubbish behind for me to clean up. The kids were all still out in the bush on the Monday, so I rolled up my sleeves and set about cleaning and getting the shed ready for the new term.

I was now down to a more manageable twenty-two students, and on our first day we set about cleaning the school properly and splashing paint around, literally. We started going to the main school to watch educational movies and for sports days, going on to compete against the convent school at various sporting competitions. Sports uniforms were made by parents at the night school, and by me and the students doing home science subjects.

That first Tuesday was a great day in the Pindan mob's history. Twelve of the little kids were going into Grade 1 at the main school. Tony Barker, the new school principal, had suggested they go for an initial visit on the Tuesday morning, to see how they liked it before starting full time. On the Tuesday morning, they were all very happy and excited and not in the least bit shy, barging into the classroom to join in the morning talks. They stayed quite happily.

The infant's teacher did not get on all that well with all my little kids. She was unable to hold their interest, and one or two misbehaved when her back was turned. I couldn't quite believe it when I found out—they had been perfect with me—but one little boy, the same little fellow who had been the first to admit to eating a cupcake the previous term, ended up coming back to the Loco Shed for the year. He became a bit of a mascot with the bigger kids, who would take turns putting him on their shoulders when we were on class expeditions. The other littlies all settled in at PHSS, and all at the staging school were ready to learn. I was so proud of and for them.

One of the first things Tony Barker asked me at the start of the year was if any of my kids wanted to go to the annual North West Camp School. He suggested we choose those who could speak and understand English the best, and I went to ask the Two Mile Elders. Daisy Bindi was the most concerned, because of her memories of kids being taken in what we now call the 'Stolen Generations'. She and some of the parents were worried that they wouldn't come back. It was decided by the mob that the staging school kids wouldn't go.

I had brought back with me from Perth a fair bit of manual training equipment to help the older kids with their trade skills, and Friends there had donated fifty pounds, a huge amount of money at the time, to help buy equipment and supplies as needed. The staging school was adopted by the local Rotary Club and they provided great assistance, as did other Rotary Clubs.

However, new opportunities for the Two Mile students could also bring problems. I was excited when they were invited to join in the PHSS's swimming lessons, but no one had any bathers or swimmers to wear. Once again, I put out the call to my wonderful mother, Friends in Perth and now the local Rotary Club for help. The bathers were an urgent addition to a long list of items we could use in both home science and manual training classes—strong cheap fabric, empty tins, any cutlery, tin openers, saucepans, mixing bowls, cups, measuring jugs and scissors. To my absolute delight, almost everything we requested seemed to arrive in a short time. Support from all of these generous people helped dispel any doubt in my mind that what I was doing wasn't appreciated.

The big 'boys' from the previous year were working at harvesting pearl shell as planned, though they still attended night school with the other adults. My big girls had been given a choice at the start of the school year—husbands or school. Nearly all the big girls came back, including Djilila, despite her having given birth to her baby boy, Phillip, on Christmas Day. Phillip then became a teaching resource. We held mothercraft and fathercraft sessions, with lessons coming up by correspondence from the Perth Infant Health Centre, and Phillip's dad would also come along to the school and teach leather plaiting. Practical teaching at its best.

One of my lovely fourteen-year-old girls didn't come back. She was missing from school, and when I asked the others where she was I was told she was at the camp. I went over that afternoon after school and saw a large number of people in a circle with the girl sitting in the middle. Someone went in and grabbed her hair and punched her in the face, and this was then repeated by others. I asked Peter Coffin what was going on, and he explained that she had shamed her family by playing around with a boy who had the wrong skin name for her. He then explained that only her family were allowed to punish her, no one else, or there would be payback. But it was all too late; she was already pregnant.

~

The combined state school and the staging school played the convent school in a softball competition. Our boys won, but the girls lost. Softball took the place of our version of tennis, both in the playground and at Two Mile. I thought softball a better game, as it took more organising and more leadership than the simple game of 'tennis' we played at school. It was interesting to see whom they elected as captain for each game at Two Mile, compared with whom I chose at school. I'm not certain, but I think their choice was more to do with skin relations than leadership.

Night classes were going well. My students would walk over the hill or the older ones would arrive in a taxi or some old bomb that was often on its last legs. Sometimes I'd arrive after basketball practice and find the night school students sitting around outside singing corroboree songs as they waited for me. It was a wonderful welcome. I felt it was very worthwhile spending my time teaching them as well as the kids.

Both Peter and Ernie told me at various times that they didn't like to talk about the literacy classes to the rest of the Pindan mob; they feared that they'd all come to Two Mile, wanting to learn to read and write, but there simply wasn't enough work there for them all. I didn't realise it at the time, but this was probably the first sign of unrest in the mob. Later on, that would directly impact the school, me and the kids.

At one night class, Ernie and Peter came and asked if I'd take head shots of them both with my camera and send them off for processing as soon as possible. They were both applying for Citizenship Rights.

In 1960 Aboriginal people were not regarded as citizens. In applying, Ernie and Peter had to prove that they were free from disease, could speak English, had been 'civilised' in behaviour for two years, could manage their affairs, were industrious in their habits and, finally, that they had severed all ties with their Aboriginal family and friends. I took the photos and sent them down to Perth for processing. The applications were sent in as soon as the photos came back.

Ernie was granted citizenship. He had received a reference from my supervisor, Mr Rourke, and my father, and Ernie became the first of his mob to receive Australian citizenship. I'm uncertain if, or when, Peter attained his.

Citizenship for all Aboriginal people wasn't granted until after a national referendum held in 1967. The referendum called for an amendment of the Australian Constitution, namely the removal of parts of two sections (shown in bold type below):

*Section 51, Part (xxv1): The Parliament shall, subject to this Constitution, have power to make laws for the peace, order, and good government of the Commonwealth with respect to:- The people of any race, **other than the aboriginal race in any state**, for whom it is deemed necessary to make special laws*

*Section 127: In reckoning the numbers of the people of the Commonwealth, or of a State or other part of the Commonwealth, **aboriginal natives should not be counted.***

By removing these two phrases from the Constitution, Indigenous Australians were granted citizenship, and included in the population. Of the Australian voting public at the time, 5,183,113 people voted in favour, and only 527,007 voted against.

40

NEEDLES AND THREADS

My wonderful mother sent up a bolt of sturdy white material so the girls could have their first sewing lessons on our three hand-powered sewing machines, but first they practised sewing straight lines on pieces of paper. The lines needed to be perfectly straight and one inch (2.5 centimetres) apart.

On our first try, we ended up with two broken needles. One of them was broken in three places and lodged in a girl's finger, resulting in a trip to the doctor and no spare needles. Not the best of starts.

We went on to make a wide variety of items: baby clothes for expectant mothers at the camp; handkerchiefs; white aprons for cooking classes; dozens of navy-blue pants for the small girls; and peasant skirts, which were fashionable at the time. Some of the girls became proficient at creating beautiful fancywork (embroidery).

We would often have visitors from the camp call in to see the school and we would serve them tea in our often mismatched china tea set, placed on our embroidered tablecloth and all.

Our cooking repertoire had expanded from porridge and packet cakes to cupcakes, scones, rock cakes, sausage rolls, jam tarts, custard, stews and eventually a three-course meal. All the food was shared and enjoyed between us, and with visitors whenever they called in.

The manual training students created tables, bookcases and benches out of packing cases, putting both their newfound woodworking and metalworking skills to use around the Loco Shed. My Uncle Ralph's church men's group also sent up packs for the manual training students to put together to make sets of kindergarten size chairs and tables. We set up rosters and the kids took turns cleaning the shed; they had pride in their work, and I was very proud of them. It was worth it for me to work as an usherette, and for all of us to clean the school, so we could share the experience of seeing their creations evolve, be consumed and be utilised.

As well as for sport and educational films, we were asked to the main school for all school assemblies. It was wonderful seeing the kids integrating into PHSS, accepting and being accepted. There was sometimes shyness or reserve, especially at the start, but it never lasted long.

As part of PHSS, we were invited to the upcoming Pilbara District Inter School Sports Day, to be held at Wittenoom, 128 miles (206 kilometres) due south, on the June long weekend. All the children were to be billeted with different families. In preparation, I started teaching the kids how to eat with cutlery, as well as 'white' table and personal manners, saying 'please' and 'thank you', which was all relatively easy. The principal, Mr Barker, was a bit concerned that the kids wouldn't know how to behave, so we asked him and some of the older PHSS kids out for a meal. We set tables and cooked up a three-course meal for us all, and Mr Barker left satisfied after watching them eat and behave the entire time.

There was then a mad scramble to find enough pyjamas for all the Two Mile kids, so I sent another urgent request to Friends in Perth. Next was making sure all of the kids had white shorts that fitted, and then sewing a blue stripe down each side, to wear with white tops—the PHSS sports uniform. The night school sewing ladies helped, and each of the girls who were learning sewing picked a white blouse to sew for themselves, rather than the white singlets the boys would be wearing.

Having organised this, I knew my next step in getting the kids to Wittenoom would be asking Daisy Bindi to agree to letting the kids go. Thankfully we still had a couple of months to talk it all through.

41

TOMMY

I first got to meet the old man Tommy Sampi in Port Hedland after the Easter break. I knew that in 1946 he had started a bush school for the kids impacted by the strike. I also knew that Dad had met him previously, because I'd seen a photo of him in our photo album.

On the day I met him, Tommy had been drinking and he was out the back of Elders raving about the hellfire that all his people were going through. He told my landlord, Jack Glass, to collect some kids and 'givem ejucashun'. Jack then introduced him to me.

Although Tommy was drunk, I think being introduced to me almost shocked him into sobriety. I told him my father had a photo of him with the school kids at Yandiyarra; he corrected me, 'You wrong—Twelve Mile!' Then something—maybe my name and the reference to the photo—must have clicked in his brain.

'Ah, Miss Gare,' he said, 'I come to your school tomorrow. You spare me a few hours. I know your father. Oh,

Miss Gare, I meet you too sudden,' he stammered. 'Your father—Christmas toys.' Then he started to sob with loud noises and much blubbering as he clung on to me.

I got carried away with the emotion as well and nearly started up alongside him, but then I realised all the workers and customers were watching, so I told him to come to the school in the morning when he felt better. I assumed the Christmas toys he had referred to would probably have been gifts from Friends in Perth that my father had passed on to him.

Years later I came across a copy of a letter Dad had written in 1947, while he was up north with the Native Welfare Council. He had met Don McLeod, Tommy and some of the other strikers. In the letter to Don, he said he'd been asked to do a few talks with interested people, including the Native Rights committee, but he felt rather presumptuous after only spending a few days in the Kimberley and the Pilbara with the strikers.

He reassured Don that there was a strong desire to know and appreciate the viewpoint of Aboriginal people, but that there were very few prepared or willing to describe the situation. 'The native question,' he wrote, 'like all questions from the North, are very remote to the general public here [Perth]. How do we get action and not words? Education can be administered like castor oil or it can be inculcated by desire, the only successful way I think, and Tom Sampi seems to be right on track there. I had a talk with the correspondence people and told them of Tommy's work, I hope the service will give him lessons to help. Our policy [Native Welfare Council] is to work with the government in any way possible, but it is hard work when there are no pressure votes for an MP to consider.'

I was amazed. Had Dad instilled these thoughts in me as a child, twelve years before? He and I certainly had discussions about his visits north, but I would have only been eleven years of age in 1947. I know that I talked about becoming a teacher, as I loved school and my teachers at Darlington Primary. It was his description of how to administer education, through desire, that surprised me, because this was indeed how I was teaching. Kids need to want to learn, irrespective of the colour of their skin.

~

Tommy Sampi came to the staging school the following day and he was an altogether different man from the one I had met the day before. He would probably have beaten me at a vocabulary test, and he was very serious. He told me the history of his school at Twelve Mile and how Dad had been his first visitor, and the trouble he had had obtaining the correspondence lessons.

Tommy wrote a letter to the state Education Department in late 1946, asking for correspondence material to help him educate the kids at his bush school. A few months later an inspector was sent out to Twelve Mile by the director of education. He questioned Tommy's ability to teach beyond infant class; he reported that there was not a stable population at the camp and that the permanence of the school was in doubt due to dissention in the camp. Subsequently no correspondence lessons were sent to Twelve Mile and, despite Tommy trying to continue to teach with a handful of old picture books, the school was eventually disbanded. His school had been a big thing for him, and some of the kids he had taught were now the parents of my kids.

Before he left the Loco Shed, he told me that when Dad visited them, he had told Tommy that he had a daughter who wanted to be a teacher, and that he would send her up to teach Aboriginal people. Dad certainly went up in Tommy's esteem after he met me and saw the kids getting on so well at our school. He also told me that the Two Mile mob might seem okay when they talk to me, but I must understand that they had reason to doubt any government workers because of what the government had done to them by taking their children.

When Tommy was at Port Hedland, he was staying at the One Mile camp and he helped my only student from there with his reading. After he'd visited our school, I heard that he apparently held an impromptu meeting at Two Mile to tell the kids and adults that they could trust me and that it was a good school. He also told them that I wouldn't kidnap their kids or turn them against the adults.

The next visitor to the school was Daisy Bindi, beautifully dressed, earrings and all. The kids thrilled her by standing and saying, 'Good morning, Daisy', just as they did for all visitors. She nodded and said, 'That's good.' She had come to show me a page in a magazine about her visit to Perth with the strikers. It was quite good, and I read it to the kids when she was there, while drumming into them pride in their heritage.

Daisy asked if she could take the kids into the bush for the weekend. I told her that as long as they didn't miss any school, then it was all right by me, but that actually it was nothing to do with me—it was up to Peter and Ernie. I found out later that they were scared that if she took them out, she wouldn't bring them back; but during her visit she kept assuring me over and over that this would not happen, which puzzled me at the time.

Don McLeod had apparently come back to Two Mile. When I asked about this, Daisy told me that she had thanked him for all his help, but now she wanted him to leave them alone. She said she was against his idea of moving them to Roebourne, which was two hundred kilometres down the coast, and she'd told Don that she would not allow it. This was all news to me and I listened with interest, trying to work out how this might impact on the upcoming sports weekend at Wittenoom.

A taxi driver arrived at the Loco Shed to take Daisy into town, and so I asked if he'd like to join us for a cup of tea, which he readily accepted. Was he surprised! Tea and biscuits with Daisy and me—a tablecloth, our prettiest china tea set, and all.

42

DASH TO DERBY

I had quite a lot to do with the MMA staff who lived in, and flew in and out of, Port Hedland. If nothing else because I'd pick up freight parcels that would arrive from my parents and others in Perth. Most of the staff were young and good fun, and they all knew of my connection with their boss, my father.

One Saturday in early June, when I heard that one of the hosties, Marian, had had a nasty accident near the aerodrome, I went out to check. She had been riding a scooter that didn't have any oil left in it and the engine had seized as she was riding at about sixty-five kilometres per hour, throwing her off. She was lucky to suffer only cuts and bruises, but she was very stiff and sore. She was supposed to be doing the next flight to Derby, but she was unable to, and later flew back to Perth to convalesce.

The boss of MMA Port Hedland was going to be Marian's replacement, but when I said how lucky he was, it was suggested that I could do it instead. I told him that I had to be back by Sunday afternoon, so it was agreed that if I helped out, they'd get me back in time. I immediately donned a uniform, but there were no spare hats, so I tied a scarf around my head, looking a bit like a washerwoman, and went to the drome to wait for the plane.

When the plane came in, I explained to Judy, the hostess who had just come in on the flight, what had happened. She thanked me and headed off the tarmac. I realised then that I would be the only hostess on the flight and, despite seeing the hosties look after passengers many times, I realised I wouldn't know what I was doing or where anything was!

Thankfully, Judy came back to me and said she'd been told to come too. We had a whale of a time. There were only eight passengers, including Mac, one of MMA's people, so there was much cheek, thrills and spills. We arrived at Derby late on the Saturday afternoon, and it was organised that I would fly back at one on the following afternoon, after staying the night at the MMA hostel.

Mac took Judy and me to the pub for a squash, and on the Sunday morning I caught up with the Derby schoolteachers, then with Bishop Frewer and three girls from Forrest River who had been in Girl Guides there and happened to be in Derby for the weekend. Bishop had recently been to Forrest River and gave me all the gossip. Louisa was now the village baker and she baked all the bread, which was then sold through the store. Seeing Bishop and looking at his recent photos of the red earth and the boab trees, and after talking with the Forrest River girls, I remembered my promise to myself. Now more than ever, I wanted to go back there again.

I arrived back in Hedland in time for a 'do' at the school. We had a visitor from the Claremont Rotary Club, who was presenting us with a box of goods for the school. It is amazing how much people will give when you ask; the school was now well stocked, mostly with second-hand goods, but these new donations would all find good use. One of the bigger kids gave a short speech of thanks, and then we took our visitor on a tour of the school and showed him some of the work we were doing.

Derby had been a wonderful short distraction from Port Hedland and the trouble that seemed to be brewing at Two Mile.

43

WITTENOOM

The pyjamas arrived just in time, amid much excitement. We had so many that, once I had allocated a pair to each child who we hoped would be going to the sports day in Wittenoom, I had plenty to give out to the other non-team members at the school.

We were still to get Daisy Bindi's permission to take the kids for the weekend, and it took a lot to convince her that we were not stealing the children. I was part of the government as far as she was concerned, and the government took children away. This trip to Wittenoom, she feared, might be just the starting point.

Tommy had given me some useful pointers, and I silently thanked him for that. I explained to her how the whole trip would work and what a great opportunity it would be for the kids. I made a list for her of all the kids' names and I explained again where they were going and what they would be doing. I wrote her name on the top of the list and dated it. It felt like I had signed a receipt for them before we left, and she told me firmly that she was going to count the kids when they arrived back.

Not understanding properly the enormous impact of the stolen generation events, I told her she had hurt me by not trusting me and that I was sad. Then she became worried and told me how pleased she was with the school. The kids were eventually allowed to go to the Pilbara District Inter School Sports Day at Wittenoom, but Daisy was keeping a firm eye on it all.

Wittenoom had been built in the 1940s specifically for the employees of the local blue asbestos mine, and at the time it was the largest inland town in the North West, with about nine hundred inhabitants living and working there. Like Port Hedland, Wittenoom had two schools, the state school and a Catholic school.

Both of the trips, down and then back, were hectic. To start with, we piled one hundred Port Hedland kids—sixty from the Port Hedland state and staging schools, and forty from the local convent school—into three trucks on the Saturday of the June long weekend. The sports day would be held on the Sunday, and we would travel back on the Monday. The staging school kids were in white shorts; the boys wore Port Hedland State School singlets with 'PHSS' stencilled across the front, and the girls wore the pretty white blouses we had made for Steve Wallace's visit the previous December.

I was in charge of forty-five girls on the back of one truck. Talk about a jam. We were squished in there for the 188-mile (303-kilometre) journey along mostly dirt roads. I had to set a good example, so I sat up and smiled while sitting on my knees with my lower legs tucked up beneath me as we bounced and lurched along the road.

We stopped once on the way to have a rest and a much-needed stretch. We gave the kids an apple each to snack on, and a drink. I remember the beautiful bright-red Sturt Desert peas were out in flower beside the road, which we all admired before climbing back up and continuing on our long trip. A few were sick but, being kids, they soon got over it and, despite this, said they enjoyed themselves. I was certainly glad to see the end of that bumpy trip.

The Wittenoom town greeted our arrival at 4.30 p.m., with the kids all being billeted with different families, some meeting up again at the outdoor pictures that night. Asbestos tailings were used everywhere, like other places would use gravel—to surface roads, paths and the local racecourse. The local kids used to play in piles of tailings around the town. I remember thinking how good it was that the roads were so smooth. I, like most people at the time, had no understanding of the lung disease (mesothelioma) and slow death that lay in that innocuous-looking blue dust.

On the Sunday morning, all the kids lined up in their school groups, tallest at the front. Five schools were present—two from Port Hedland, two from Wittenoom and one from Marble Bar. There would have been six if you'd counted the staging school separately. I remember thinking that the whole event must have been quite a feat to organise. The girls were set apart from the boys, and then they were further broken down into age groups. Most of the white kids wore sports shoes with their uniforms; the Pindan kids were barefoot, but it certainly didn't hinder them or their spirit.

The staging school kids had an outstanding day, the boys doing slightly better than the girls. Fourteen-year-old Tommy Gardner took out championship trophies in both high jump and long jump. He jumped 18'7" (5.66 metres) in the long jump, and in the high jump, as the other competitors fell by the wayside, he cleared the bar every time, right up to 5'5" (165 centimetres). He possibly could have jumped higher, but there were no more holes left in the posts!

It was an incredible feat in itself, but all the Pindan kids had their own style, running straight towards the bar and tucking their knees up under their chins as they jumped. I can remember thinking, as I watched Tommy, 'Imagine how high he could go if he had been taught the other way!' Another of the boys was so far ahead of the other competitors in the long distance race that he looked back and waited for the others to catch up before starting to run again. And he still won.

The Wittenoom headmaster asked Tony Barker, who had also accompanied our kids, if the Pindan kids could put on a dance display that night. Tony thought they would be too tired, but he still asked me. The kids were so excited when I asked them. They had done so well in the competitions that I think they would have done anything for anyone. So we got some lime for paint, found a pipe for a didgeridoo, lit a fire and rolled a tyre onto it. The kids were rather taken aback by the crowd—over three hundred people—but, still, they thrilled everyone and we finished with a few songs in English, including 'It's a Long Way to Tipperary'.

It was all over in three-quarters of an hour. The whole time, there were cameras flashing. The final item was 'Waltzing Matilda', for which I asked everyone to join in; then I made a speech thanking Wittenoom for their organisation and hospitality, and the Wittenoom headmaster gave a reply. I was so happy for my kids; they had had quite a day.

The following day, those people who had billeted the Pindan kids raved to me about their manners and cleanliness. They hadn't expected anything like it. One couple, who had no children of their own, had asked for five Aboriginal kids; they got six, and were warned by 'well-wishers' in the town that the kids would be dirty, lousy and dishonest. But when I thanked the wife for looking after them and said goodbye, she was crying; she told me she had loved having them and how sad she was that they were going. Among themselves, the kids were calling their billeters 'Mummy' and 'Daddy', and they all said they'd had a wonderful time.

When we returned to school on Tuesday, the kids wrote thank-you letters, which included thanks for the good food, the oranges and soft beds. It had been an adventure for them on so many levels.

The Wittenoom mine was shut down in 1966, just six years later. Fibro was by then no longer a popular insulation product, and the awareness was growing around the world of the deadly respiratory diseases caused by the fine asbestos fibres. Wittenoom was de-gazetted by the Western Australian government and is now a ghost town. Nonetheless, it is still visited by curious tourists, despite the warning signs about the dangers of asbestos posted outside the once-thriving town.

44

McLEOD'S MOB

Before school started on the Monday after our visit to Wittenoom, I had a visit from both Ernie and Peter warning me about anyone who might come to the school saying they 'owned' one of my students and wanting to take them away. Apparently Don McLeod's mob, those who had not broken away or sent their children to Port Hedland with Ernie and Peter, were trying to take the kids away from the school. Ernie said that the only real parents anywhere nearby were his mob, and that they wanted the kids to stay at the school. Whew, what was I in for?

Daisy then came down to the school the following day and told me that the parents were coming on Saturday to take all of their fourteen-year-old kids. She told me that Ernie's mob were not looking after them properly. She spoke of the girl who had become pregnant during the Christmas holidays, and told me that the previous Monday four boys had been fined by the local police for receiving liquor. She was going to send them back to the bush so that the government couldn't take them and they would be able to look after their old people, as that was the only duty of all young people.

I sympathised with her, but I explained that if she took all of the big kids, I would be down to only nine students and the school would have to close. She just laughed and told me, 'They're going to leave, I tell you. I'm cunnin'. Guvment never bin help us black fellas before and we can get on all right without 'em now.'

I asked about their child endowment and pensions, which they wouldn't receive if they went bush, and she replied, 'We'll manage.' I knew that they could, but felt sad that the kids would not get the education Ernie's mob wanted. After she left, I started to think about what I would do for a living from the next week onwards.

Daisy was determined, and she was the type of person who once she had an idea will fight for it to the end. Unfortunately for her, because she had changed sides several times between the now two mobs—Don's and Ernie's—few at Two Mile camp were listening to her.

I saw Biddy Coffin at the pictures the following night and she told me there had been a big argument about the kids the night before. Ernie had gone to the police; he had told Don and Daisy that they were not the kids' real parents and they could not take the kids. Ernie said that if they had good food and a school, he wouldn't mind, but Don couldn't guarantee anything. I knew Daisy would be mad.

I went out and met Don McLeod at the Two Mile camp and asked him if he wanted to come over to the school. He said something like, 'No way. I won't have anything to do with that place, that's against all my ideas.' That did take me back a little, but there was no changing his mind.

That weekend there was a big meeting at Two Mile to decide whether it was Ernie or Don who was going to lead the co-op company that had been established when the Pindan mob first decided to pool their resources. Ernie told me before the meeting that if Don was chosen, then he would get out with his mob and form another company.

It looked like there was no hope of them all coming together again, and I felt sorry for them; they all thought they were doing what was best for their mob.

45

ERNIE'S MOB

I was surprised when Ernie and a ute full of men pulled up in town to see me on the weekend of the big meeting. Ernie looked furious and stated that I had double-crossed him. I had no idea what he was talking about.

It turned out that at the meeting Daisy had produced a piece of paper, which Ernie now thrust at me. It was the list, in my handwriting, of all the kids who went to Wittenoom, with her name on the top—the list I'd given her before she'd allowed the kids to go to the inter school sports day. She had told the meeting that it was authority from me for her to take all the kids. Don let her speak and they believed her.

When Ernie showed me the list and I explained what it was, they roared with laughter and then headed straight back out to the meeting. But I was cross with Daisy.

Daisy, egged on by Don, had become a nuisance at the school. It was all becoming a dreadful mess, and I felt that the staging school kids were caught in the middle. The Monday morning after the meeting, she tried to stop some of the kids

SALLY GARE with FREDA MARNIE

from coming to school, but Ernie ordered the kids to ignore her and go off. She threatened that she would just come down and take them. Don then turned up at the school and tried to take one of the boys, but he howled, yelled and put on such a fuss that Don let him go.

It was an awkward position to be placed in as their teacher. My responsibility for the kids when they were at school was being directly challenged. Don continued to refuse to come into the Loco Shed, and he told me that when someone says to him 'You can't take the kids', they were just asking him to do it. He then stated that he was putting the whole matter before the United Nations and he would shame Western Australia before the whole world. He left without any of the kids.

Settling the kids down and concentrating on our work was a challenge after that, but we continued on. I had no idea what to expect next.

That afternoon Ernie, Peter and another breakaway strike leader, 'Coombie', came over to the school with Mr Griffin— a white man from Perth who was company secretary of the Pindan co-op—to fill me in on developments. The weekend had been momentous for the Two Mile mob; in a vote at their board meeting, Ernie had come out on top and it had been decided that he would lead the company. Don was packing up and going to Roebourne, apparently for good, but he was still trying to take as many as possible with him. Basically, the Two Mile mob had decided they wanted to stay and educate their kids.

Over the next few days, it didn't get much better. I was told that Peter and Ernie were in Perth on company business; Don was supposed to have gone to Roebourne, but I then heard he was still in Hedland, apparently waiting for any opportunity to 'steal' the children.

Having had enough, I asked Tony Barker to come and see Don McLeod with me. We spent two and a half hours with him and persuaded him to visit inside the staging school. At first he wouldn't—the outside was shameful enough for him, he said—but he relented and came in to have a look.

I remember Don's look of complete surprise, almost incredulousness, when he looked in at the school. We had the desks in rows, we had the kids' works everywhere. It was a real school, with Aboriginal culture incorporated. I told him how the old men in camp taught leatherwork and shell carving, as well as white fellas in town coming out and teaching mechanics and carpentry. I explained that we had to teach the school curriculum—the reading, writing and maths—but as the little kids moved into the state school, we taught the older kids trades, and they could attend the night school with other adults. He actually congratulated me, but I wasn't allowed to bask in this glory for long.

He read us a letter from an ex-preacher in Melbourne who had joined the Victorian Education Department; he asked for further particulars about a teaching job Don had offered him. Similar to his previous attempts, Don's idea was that this man would wander around with them and teach the kids only what Don agreed they should learn. The ex-preacher seemed quite excited about the idea and was going to come over to Western Australia for six weeks during the Christmas holidays to try it out. If he liked it, he would stay; if not, he would go back to Melbourne without obligation.

Don still maintained that the price being paid for the education at Two Mile was too great; that price being that the kids were living with Ernie's mob in the Port Hedland environment, with its grog, swearing and unmarried mothers.

Mr Middleton, the Western Australian Commissioner of Native Affairs, then intervened, telling Don that he, Mr Middleton, was solely responsible for any 'native' child, above even its parent. He quoted Section 8 of the Western Australian *Aborigines Act 1905*: 'The Chief Protector shall be the legal guardian of every aboriginal and half-caste child until such child attains the age of sixteen years.' Mr Middleton said that if he thought they would be better off with Don in the bush he would let them go, but he was satisfied that Two Mile was the proper place for them.

Two days after Tony and I visited Don, I received a long letter from him, saying in part 'the reintroduction by Middleton of Section 8, a very harsh and inhuman measure which significantly was retained when over half the old act was deleted in 1955, recreates the old situation as the result of which over three hundred children have been spirited away from the district in earlier years and apart from one girl, the sister of Patrick who was a pupil in your school before Christmas not one other has ever been heard of by their families. The history of Patrick's sister has little to recommend it since although married in due course she subsequently ran away with another white man to Melbourne. With this background it is felt that the decision to steal any of the children as and when opportunity offers should be the right course for already there is evidence of the fact that the bigger boys are intolerant of discipline.'

I felt like crying in sympathy with Don. After all his work and his achievements alongside these people—helping them become sustainable without government help, while retaining their traditional ways—he'd now been voted out and he couldn't find a way back.

Don left for Roebourne, and two of my students 'disappeared'. One was a child of his mob, but the other one was an eight-year-old whose parents were both living with Ernie's mob. Not long after, Daisy also went to Roebourne and took one of the thirteen-year-old boys with her. She called him her Granny (grandchild), based on his skin name. His mother had passed away, and his father worked for Ernie Mitchell's mob near Jigalong. It was a dreadful feeling going to school each morning and wondering how many more kids had disappeared overnight. No more did, and ultimately the eight-year-old came back.

Ernie arrived back from Perth and was very disappointed with what had happened. He and Peter had been to Perth for a court case against Don, but Don hadn't turned up. The co-operative apparently had debts of about four thousand pounds at the time. They had agreed to supply seven thousand tonnes of manganese from their mine near Marble Bar, the profits from which would clear the debt. There was also interest from other mining companies to help the Pindan co-operative expand and modernise the mine, so formalising the leadership change became important. However, I'm not sure whether the expansion ever eventuated.

The staging school continued on, and we didn't hear anything more from Don. I never saw Daisy Bindi again but heard that she had a lower leg amputation due to complications from her diabetes and that she died the following year. She had been a strong woman for her mob.

46

LOW TIDE

With the weather improved, we continued to go down to the beach for lessons. As the tide went out, it would expose a reef beyond the sandy shoreline. One time the low tide was so far out, and our concentration was so focused on everything that had been exposed on the reef, that we were caught out. There was a substantial gale blowing as the tide came rushing in. Keeping an eye out for stingrays and sharks, some of which we spotted, we fought against the tide as we tried to get back to the sandbank, a strip of hard sand that led back to shore but was now lying under water. All very exhilarating, with many stories to write about.

We had a six-year-old boy arrive; his father, Clancy McKenna, had been one of the first to lead the strike with Don McLeod back in 1946, and Clancy had recently been imprisoned for three months for drinking and bad behaviour. The little boy had originally been sent to the main school, but he fought there and swore, spat and stole, so they sent him out to me to be 'staged'. I put him under the care of the naughtiest boy to mentor and look after, and the change in both of them was instantaneous. They were both bright and active, but they behaved like angels in class.

Claremont Teachers College had donated to the school an old wind-up gramophone player with a battery-powered speaker, plus some gramophone records for children, a few of which were scratched, but it didn't matter too much as long as we could play them. Another great learning tool, as there were many excellent recordings for kids around at that time. *Popeye* became a favourite, as was *Little Toot* with the younger ones.

Both the school and camp were hit by a flu epidemic, and I also contracted it, losing a lot of weight. At its height we only had six kids turn up at school; we tried to get through the day—everyone sniffling and coughing, including me—but I ended up sending them home for the afternoon. The local doctor came out not long after to take a look at all of the kids; he diagnosed widespread trachoma and anaemia, resulting in a blanket treatment for trachoma and a year-round dose of iron tablets to be dished out at school.

The dentist then came out to examine the kids' teeth and found that the eight oldest kids all had their wisdom teeth— so they were at least sixteen years of age, and possibly up to twenty years of age! That meant that last year's 'boys', who looked noticeably older, were probably as old as, or older than, I was.

~

The winter months in Hedland were always milder than freezing Perth, and the town was buzzing. The annual horse racing carnival was coming up.

At this time, Aboriginal and Torres Strait Islander peoples were still not classified as citizens and they were not allowed to purchase alcohol, but there were unscrupulous white men who would buy alcohol and sell it on at a profit to any Aboriginal people who could afford it. Ernie was concerned about the impact on the camp with the upcoming influx of visitors and alcohol.

There was great excitement in the classroom, as there would be a merry-go-round in town and an amusement arcade running alongside the pub. I was quite excited, but most of the locals couldn't see why, some of the old timers labelling it all a bloody nuisance.

The Cubs ran a cool drinks and refreshment stall to raise funds; I busied myself making out a roster and supporting them over the weekend. But some of Ernie's fears about the races and alcohol came to fruition, and a punishment session ensued the Monday afterwards. I only found out about it because I went out to the camp after very few of my kids turned up to school on Monday, to see how many adults would be coming to night school.

There was a crowd of about a hundred people sitting in a rough circle around one young fellow. Peter Coffin met me and said, 'We're straightening all these young blokes up. They're all breaking our law.'

I asked him in what way. 'Grog and taking their pick of a mate. Causes too much fighting and it's goin' 'gainst our law. This picking and choosing is all right, but they can't break the law. Sergeant [the local police sergeant] came out and told us this Pindan law is one hundred per cent and we don't want to get spoiled by visitors before races next time.'

I asked him what was happening to the poor fellow in the middle, who was one of my young night school men. 'He's not proper man yet and he bin playin' around with the young girls. All his relations, and anyone who likes to, can go in and hit him, shake him, yell at him and tell him off. We make him feel really shamed. If they hang their head down, someone yanks it up again. He got to look up.'

Next, I asked Peter if the bad one was allowed to speak. 'Oh, Jesus yes. If he can explain himself, we really pleased. But usually he knows if Ernie calls his name, he's guilty all right and everyone knows it. No one trying to break out. We give 'em rough time for 'bout half an hour, then tell 'em how many weeks' punishment, and not to do it again.' He then explained that someone other than a relative at the camp is put in charge of the punishment. They can boss that person round and make him/her work hard all day.

I saw one woman who had started on her punishment. She was carrying two heavy buckets of water and was followed by another older woman who was in charge of her. I recalled how one of my day school girls had been through the mill for chasing a boy who was 'not straight' for her. The poor girl had asthma all the next day, but other than that the telling off didn't seem to hurt her.

The punishment meeting went all afternoon and didn't finish until after midnight. The mob still hadn't settled down after the races, and the following day I had to go and round up some of the kids, only to find some of them had snuck off to the Roebourne Races.

47

TOM

The kids and I eventually settled back into our usual routine at school. At the beginning of one school day, a young Public Works Department engineer came into the shed to collect supplies just as we were starting our morning song and dance. I could see him watching, fascination spreading across his face as the kids and I danced to the accompaniment of the didgeridoo and clapsticks. He came around, introduced himself and asked if he could return and audio-tape us. I agreed.

He raced back to where he was living and returned with a tape recorder and recorded a session. He then invited me to his place that night, to hear it and enjoy a home-cooked meal. I agreed, thinking I could play the recording later for the kids and the Two Mile mob; I was quietly impressed that he could cook. What followed was probably one of the most painful gastronomic experiences of my life.

That night we listened to the recording, which was quite good, and then he produced an incredible-smelling curry for us to eat. It certainly didn't look or smell like any curry powder-infused meal I had eaten before. This was swiftly confirmed, as my mouth, my tongue—it felt like even my teeth—were on fire as I chewed and swallowed. And that was the first mouthful! I felt it would be impolite not to eat what he prepared for me, so slowly, painfully, I ate what had been put before me. My lips, mouth, gullet and stomach were burning—but I made it.

We chatted over the meal, with me trying not to show my discomfort too much. He told me he had seen me back in March or April on the Port Hedland jetty, where he was overseeing the jetty reconstruction. As he strolled onto the jetty, I had been walking back along it with a chaff bag full of three large Spanish mackerel over my shoulder, which he had helped me with. This done, I apparently strapped them onto my Lambretta and took off without a word of thanks. Not very appreciative of me.

He then reminded me that we had actually been introduced before—at a Scout meeting in town that I'd attended with Peter Nolan. This I did suddenly remember, mostly because when I came onto the verandah, where a group of white men were sitting, everyone rose to their feet except him. Not the best start for either of us!

Tom had been born in Germany and brought up in Thailand, hence the chilli-infused curry. By the end of 1938, just after his younger brother Michael was born, his Jewish father and Lutheran mother decided to leave Germany. They didn't think they had much time before Germany would become dangerous for a Jewish man and his young family. Tom's father, Hans, was deemed too old—he was forty-five—to get into Australia, and the queue to get into the

United States was long; so, after seeking refuge in England, the alternative choices available to them were either Siam (Thailand) or China, and they chose Siam.

Hans was employed as a storeman with the British company Bombay Burma Trading Corporation Limited (BBTCL), and was then promoted to chief accountant, utilising his actual professional training. The three Herzfeld children were Eva (who changed her name to Elizabeth), Tom and Michael; they received only a limited European education after they arrived in Thailand so, at the age of twelve, Tom was sent to boarding school in Western Australia by himself. Two years later his father died of cancer, and BBTCL generously sent lump sums so both Tom and his brother could be educated at Guildford Grammar to the end of high school. The school honoured the arrangement by seeing both boys through their schooling, despite a shortfall in funds in their final years.

After school, Tom studied engineering at the University of Western Australia and had been with the Public Works Department since graduation; he had been heavily involved with government construction throughout the North West. He was also involved with Scouts and the Church of England, so we started talking about subjects we were both interested in. Despite our earlier, somewhat abrupt, introductions to each other and the fact my burnt gullet would take time to heal, from this inauspicious beginning a steady friendship developed.

I'd gone out with a few men since arriving in Port Hedland, all very platonic. When the winter tourist season finished, I was always flush with invitations to go to the pictures or other events. I'm not sure what the ratio of men to women would have been then, but there were plenty more men than women throughout most of the North West.

I'd even received a marriage proposal just before meeting Tom—from the local Italian pest control man, even though we'd only been seeing each other a short time. Marriage to him would have meant leaving Hedland and helping him set up his own pest control business in Derby, as well as being a very loyal and house-proud wife. I would have had to leave teaching, as it was not usual for women to work after marriage then. I had made light of his proposal—and told him to wait until I grew a few months older.

Imagine my embarrassment when I saw my would-be fiancé drive past as Tom and I were walking together after a pleasant day. Thankfully, he must have been concentrating on his driving because he didn't see me, but I decided I needed to let him down gently. I was starting to develop feelings for the handsome young engineer walking beside me, even if he did insist on wearing a cravat on cooler evenings.

48

REPORTS

Tom travelled around the district frequently with work and was away from Port Hedland a lot, so we didn't see each other that often over the next few weeks. When back and not working, he had his scoutmaster activities and involvement with the church, which kept him busy. I was busy enough myself with the staging school, the night school, ushering, playing the organ for church services and helping with Guides, which had now started up.

We were both busy, but Tom wrote to me at least once a week whenever he was away. He was a terrific letter writer. I busied myself with work and looked forward to his next letter or visit.

Tony Barker would come out to the school regularly to check how we were going. He'd look through our curriculum work, but as well, we'd always try to put on a display of some sort, a song or a play the kids had made up about goings on around them.

We talked about the possibility of the Two Mile kids being involved this time in camp school in the first term of the following year and, with Ernie's agreement, we set about earning money and organising clothes for the kids who would go. The three kids chosen were very excited, and all the school busied themselves in our spare time picking buffel grass to sell. Once again, I donned a scarf around my lower face and sneezed my way around the school and camp, collecting countless small seeds with the kids. By the end of the year we had raised nearly ten pounds for each child, to cover their costs.

We prepared for the parents' day held at the end of term at the main school, where we would exhibit not only the kids' written work, arithmetic, spelling and composition but some of their handiwork as well. We finished seven metal mugs, two string bags, a folding cot, baby's nighties with intricate fancywork, tables and chairs. On the day at the main school, the boys worked on a record holder, some girls were sewing, and the other kids were doing different schoolwork activities. We sang Australian songs in our best practised singing voices, and then held a corroboree in the playground.

The school was open that night so that the parents who worked through the day could see their kids' schoolwork. It was mostly fathers, and Clancy McKenna came along after being released from Broome prison. He looked through every book and asked me to read the kids' writing to him. It was lovely to share that with him.

As 1960 came to a close, I decided to give an oral presentation of the students' school reports at the Two Mile camp, because I knew most of the camp parents would not be able to fully understand a typical written school report. I was happy with the kids' academic progress, but also their social development—most of them would look at me when replying to me and confidently say, 'Yes, Miss Gare.' Such a contrast to the old mumbled replies delivered into their chests.

So, in the last week of school, I went out to Two Mile with my reports on each of the kids. Peter gave me a rickety old chair on his verandah to sit on, and all the parents and kids gathered round in front of me. The child whose report I was reading had to come forward and hear the best and the worst. Not very psychologically sound maybe, but everyone joined in the disgust and/or praise with each report.

One or two of them were too shy to answer properly if I spoke to them, so at the end, when Peter was making his little informal speech of thanks, he said, 'You know this Miss Gare here, she like a mother to you kids. She likes you all. You all know that. You don't want to be shy with her.' I really felt as though I should have been fat and buxom, with a floury apron and hands, but it was wonderful. I felt part of a big family, particularly since my own family felt so far away.

By the December school holidays, Tom and I were both heading back to Perth for holidays. Tom promised to make contact with me, but he didn't.

49

BACK TO THE PILBARA

When it was time to return to the Pilbara, I received a letter from Tom explaining that he was being transferred to Broome to work on a water investigation program for the town. Broome lacked a potable water supply. Water for domestic use was reticulated from an artesian bore, but it was too salty for drinking or gardening. It also contained hydrogen sulphide, which smelt like bad eggs. It would linger on you after showering, which was far from pleasant. Most people relied on rainwater, which they collected off their roof and stored in water tanks, and it was jealously guarded. Potable ground water had been discovered about sixteen kilometres out of town by people exploring for oil, and Tom's job was to develop a system to get this water to town.

Tom promised to visit me whenever he was in Hedland. I headed back knowing that if this promise was anything like him supposedly catching up with me in Perth, I wouldn't see him very often. I busied myself preparing for a brand-new year.

I arrived back in Port Hedland to find it much the same, with its usual gossip and scandal. The hot holiday season, with many white wives away in Perth, seemed to have encouraged a lot of shady goings-on. There were some aspects of living in a small town I didn't particularly enjoy.

Before school started, I was invited out fishing with a few townspeople, including the couple I had stayed with when I first arrived. The wife had been away and returned with a thoroughly modern beehive hairdo that I thought looked like an oversized walnut perched on and around her head. Not that I said anything, but her husband certainly did! Despite this moment of awkwardness, we had a pretty good outing, all things considered. We first visited a buffel grass pickers' camp, and then walked on to the coast.

Unfortunately the fishing was marred for me when I caught a catfish and tried to stop it from getting back into the water. One of its poison spikes poked through the rubber on my sandshoe and into my foot. I took my shoe off and squeezed the site and everyone, including me, waited for me to start writhing about in agony. Remembering Harry Butler's warning about the barbs I was expecting the worst but, apart from feeling sick and a little faint, it was really no worse than the feeling of treading on a nail.

One of the men gave me a slug of whisky and we headed back, just as the sandflies were starting to come out. I think I was pretty lucky, as I had known of people being laid up for days after being hit by a barb. Perhaps the fish's poison glands weren't working, or I squeezed the poison out with the blood, or, more luckily, I only received a glancing blow.

I saw Tony in town the day before school started and he informed me that the Year 4 teacher, Brian Hassel, wouldn't be arriving back at PHSS for the first day of school. Since my kids were still in the bush for another day or two, I told Tony I'd help out.

With my own students and staff missing, I started the school year looking after thirty-eight students from years 3, 4 and 5 out on the town hall verandah. PHSS was short of classrooms, and the class I taught was at the town hall while they waited for the new classroom to be built. The kids and I tried to get a cool breeze on the verandah, but we ended up just feeling sweaty and salty from the hot, salt-laden afternoon wind coming off the ocean. A cyclone was looming.

Unusually, there were three cyclones formed and forming off the west coast of Western Australia. One was almost stationary over the Cocos Islands; the second was between the west coast and Christmas Island. The third had started up near Darwin and was predicted to cross the coast just north of Hedland; when it arrived, it brought high seas, hurricane winds and heavy rain all along the north coast, with easterly winds coming into Hedland as well as damage to various buildings around the town, but thankfully no loss of life.

After the cyclone had passed, I went and checked the Loco Shed. Minimal damage, other than puddles of water that had been swept in under the doors. It was, I think, the eighth and last cyclone to impact the north-west coast of Western Australia that Wet Season; if you mentioned the word 'cyclone' in town, you were told to stop swearing!

I had twenty-two kids at the start of the 1961 school year, including five lively new six-year-olds. Our class included

Djilila's baby, Phillip, and there was another baby on the way for one of my older married girls. The seven little girls who moved from the Loco School to the main school that year looked really lovely in their new starched gingham dresses that the big girls had made for them. The big girls made them take them off when they returned home; they were proud of those dresses and didn't want them to be worn day and night.

I knew the travelling superintendent from the Education Department, Mr Bainbridge, was due to visit in the first term, so when we started up in the Loco Shed, my focus became getting the kids to complete all of their written schoolwork. We still spent the same amount of time in expanding stories, but there were fewer excursions. I wanted to show the superintendent how well the kids were keeping up with the curriculum.

I decided to start up a Pindan newsletter for the Loco school; it would include stories from the kids and news of what was happening at the school, similar to what Lisa and I had created at Forrest River. The kids were excited by the idea, and we decided to call it the *Mili Mili*, which is Pindan for 'news'.

I was on the lookout to buy myself a typewriter. The state school would duplicate the newsletters for me, but I didn't think it fair to borrow their typewriter. I originally thought we'd include some of the kids' stories in their own handwriting, but I decided against it because tracing them onto the duplicating paper would ruin their wonderful work.

Bishop arrived in town and I offered to show him the school. He jumped on the back of my scooter, pulled his hat down over his ears so it wouldn't blow off, and said, 'If you go fast, Sally, I'll hang on around your waist!' We made it there in one piece, Bish laughing on the back. I couldn't help admiring the old fellow—not bad for an eighty-three-year-old.

Baby Phillip was chubby and made plenty of gurgling noises that often threatened to disrupt class, and he always laughed whenever he saw my white face. He thrilled Bish that day by rolling over with mirth when the bishop smiled at him. Bish joined in the class as the kids told us what they had been doing in the holidays, drew pictures and wrote stories. A delightful day for all of us.

Not long after Bishop's visit, Tom flew in to see me. He was on his way back down to Perth, having bought a car, a white VW Beetle, which he was planning on driving back to Broome. We talked all afternoon, and he took me out for tea at the Pier and then to the movies. We had a lovely time, and I didn't confront him about not being in contact during the school holidays, as I did not want to ruin the mood.

The following day at the aerodrome, we talked about his schedule for the next few weeks, to see when we could next meet, and his itinerary included a visit out to Forrest River. I started telling him of some of my experiences up there, and he offered to put the visit off until a school holiday period so I could go with him. I excitedly agreed—it would be wonderful to have the opportunity to go back.

I put on a slide show that night at the night school with a selection of my shots of camp school from 1957, when I had gone there with the Forrest River kids. I wanted to show them all what it was going to be like for the three Two Mile kids going. Everyone seemed to enjoy it, and it created much discussion with all the kids in the Loco Shed the following day. I was nearly as excited as the three kids who were going to go to camp school.

50

RETURN

I was playing in a basketball team in a competition against other teams in town, and after a match one night, a man from State Housing came up to me and said that the state house I had applied for back in December 1959 would soon be available. I had no idea what he was talking about. He told me we had spoken on the phone and that I had applied to him with the backing of the Education Department and Native Affairs for the use of a house as a hostel for eight teenage girls attending school in town.

I had to tell him that it wasn't me. He admitted he wasn't sure of the applicant's name. We came to the conclusion that he must have had the towns confused, but I did say that if a house became available in Port Hedland and if he couldn't find the other applicant, to please contact me.

Unfortunately, I never heard from him again, but it was strange because only that week I had said to Joy Glass that I would like a house to live in and run as a hostel for some of my students. I thought it would be for about eight kids of various ages, not just teenagers, and both boys and girls. This idea had been in the back of my mind for a while, but I certainly hadn't talked about it to anyone other than Joy.

At the end of March, Ernie and Peter asked Tony and me to go out to Two Mile to talk to all the adults about the benefits of education. When we got there, we found Peter angry and upset. Apparently, the Pindan co-op had had another big meeting and Don had threatened to send it broke by persuading all of its creditors to demand what was owed to them at the same time. There was a white man who lived at the end of the One Mile houses on the outskirts of town who would buy flour, tea and biscuits and then on-sell them to the Two Mile mob at a profit. That day, he had demanded that the co-op pay him five hundred pounds immediately or he would take them to court. Mr Griffin, the co-op's company secretary in Perth, had also written to Peter suggesting they quickly go back into running cattle, as there were still two thousand pounds owing and the debts were being called in.

Peter was worried that someone who was working with Don was angling to buy their manganese lease and that this person was behind all the 'pay up or else' business. Peter said his main worry was that the people at Two Mile were unmovable and still on a 'go-slow'. They were taking their time getting back to work after their holidays, so even if they did go back and run cattle, it wouldn't be happening in a hurry. Poor Peter was feeling so downhearted that he said he felt like resigning from the co-op. He asked us to talk not only about education and the school, and the parents' responsibility to send their kids to school, but also to stress the importance of punctuality and reliability when on a job—all the things he was worried about. Tony and I gave our talk, but we certainly weren't evangelical in our delivery.

With much excitement, we saw our three camp school kids on television that night. They had gone into the Perth television station with Harry Butler and talked about the camp. They performed a corroboree dance, which Harry later told me they'd also done at camp, where many of the other kids also learnt the songs and dance moves.

The following Monday, I was out at the Two Mile at seven in the morning to welcome back the camp school kids. All of Two Mile were sitting on the ridge waiting for the bus. There was a great rush when the bus came into sight and the mob surrounded the doorway as it pulled up. As the kids alighted the mood was solemn, with short handshakes all around and a few quiet tears from the mothers. I gave them all the day off school.

I called in several times that day and saw the camp school boys walking around, followed by the younger boys. They all walked over to the hospital and stock reserve, and then around the whole of Two Mile.

There was such a difference in these big boys at school the next day. They were bright, healthy, happy, more friendly and even more eager to learn. At morning tea they wanted to study maps, and this became a daily occurrence. As their teacher, this was a delight to see; I hoped this attitude and self-confidence would continue.

51

PARENTS & CITIZENS

The old Loco Shed was going to be replaced as our class-room, which I was in two minds about. The shed lacked basic amenities—there was no water or electricity—but it was a wonderfully large open space, where we could run both our practical classes and our normal schoolwork without having to put everything away. The brand-new facility was being erected near the Two Mile camp; it provided two class-rooms and was to be an extension of the state school. The staging school would in future have one of these classrooms, as promised previously by Steve Wallace and the Education Department. It was exciting watching it take shape and it was the subject of much morning news and story writing.

Meanwhile night school had a sudden spurt of atten-dance. I had managed to scrounge around a few more lamps to light up the big shed, and that helped. Up to then, we'd been concentrating on reading, writing and arithmetic, with a small amount of time put aside for sewing and woodwork, utilising the school equipment. But some of the mothers at Two Mile were keen to sew their own dresses, so I gave them patterns to look through and they bought their own fashionable materials. Once more I was shown, as a teacher, the value of practical learning. All of these activities unconsciously included measuring, multiplication, handling money and shopping, fractions and writing, and then writing up all their actions every night.

The night school timetable changed from mostly reading, writing and maths to one hour on these subjects and one hour on practical work. The pleasure and learning these women obtained was wonderful to see. Writing to my wonderfully supportive mother, I asked her opinion on me buying an electric sewing machine, for both the school (when we had electricity in the new classroom) and myself. I loved sewing and making my own clothes—and still do today—so I knew it would get plenty of use. The hand machines were terrific, but between night school and Loco Shed school, all three machines were in constant use, and a flash electric one would be another great learning tool.

I decided to start up our own Loco Shed parliament with the kids, to help them understand how government worked. We held a secret ballot to elect the class parliament of five members. Each elected student then had a special area of responsibility to help the school run smoothly. Health, clothing, sport and equipment, and law were four portfolios I remember, and the kids were hugely excited by it all. I thought they might have been having a bit of joke when the naughtiest boy was voted in as the Minister of Law, but yet again it demonstrated what I had seen in the past: give the disruptive child responsibility and watch them rise to the challenge. I still use this technique in adult prison work-shops to this day.

Baby Phillip was the subject of some of the news, as he had his first tooth. Never has one baby had to show his tooth to so many people. The four big boys used their woodworking tools to make a cart to pull him around in; it was a great success for both Phillip and the kids pulling him around the school.

Morning news had taken on a great new impetus as well. I offered an orange to the student who could say the most in a clear voice. The four big boys went last and, while waiting their turn, made notes on small cards that they used in their talk. Tommy won that first orange, and the next morning I tape-recorded each of them, saying we'd record them again in three weeks' time to see their improvement. When we did that, their eyes positively shone, hearing the improvement in themselves.

~

Once again, however, we were confronted by prejudice. Some vestry members (elected legal representatives of the church) had complained bitterly about 'natives' attending church and Sunday school. What I thought was most unfair was that some of these accusers didn't regularly attend service or Sunday school themselves; but they said that, when they did, they found the kids dirty and smelly. If it had been true, maybe I wouldn't have minded so much, but the kids in question lived in houses near the town and were always well kept.

The accusers just seemed to see their dark skins and imme-diately expected them to be dirty and smelly and to have runny noses. They proclaimed loudly that the mere thought of putting up with them through one of the minister's long sermons was unbearable. People used to say quite proudly at the time that there was no colour bar in Hedland—there wasn't either, just as long as the 'coloured' folk kept their distance!

This was followed by a nasty P&C (Parents & Citizens) meeting at the state school. Once again there were concerns about mixing the Aboriginal kids and white kids together in classes, particularly in the older age groups. Some of the white parents claimed that my big children were going to teach their littlies all sorts of rude things. At the time I didn't know how to reply. I couldn't very well tell them at the meeting that I had heard that their child had been lifting up the dresses of girls or had been caught passing rude drawings in school and swearing. These are all things that kids get up to on every playground, but if I compared my kids with what theirs already did, or even with these parents themselves, I'd have been put in gaol. Instead, I sat in somewhat stunned silence.

Some parents said they wouldn't come to any more P&C meetings because 'Sally Gare brings all the Pindans along'. I have always been passionate about getting parents involved with their kids' education, and I've welcomed all parents to P&C meetings and activities. This is, I feel, a vital role for teachers, and any school as a whole.

Those parents truly hurt me to tears, saying untrue things about 'my family', often without any regard or thought. I was getting to the stage where I needed a change from all the struggle. White criticism was starting to weigh on me.

Thankfully, regular letters from Tom were making me feel very supported. His letter frequency increased from one a week to two or three, and I looked forward to each and every one. Bish was prompting our romance in a none-too-subtle way. He was writing and calling in quite frequently to both of us, when he was in either Hedland or Broome, and would always tell each of us what the other had been doing for him. If ever he saw us together, he'd say, 'What's this? You're not engaged to be married, are you?'

With all the tension at P&C meetings, I decided I wanted and needed to get away for a while. I flew up to Broome for the Easter break, to visit both Bishop Frewer and Tom. Tom and I had a lovely time together and we talked about my two years at Wyndham and Forrest River Mission.

Tom had managed to move his Forrest River inspection to take place during the May school holidays. If I could get myself to Wyndham, then I could join him. I was excited at the prospect of introducing him to the beautiful scenery and people at Forrest River, and seeing them all again myself.

52

BE CAREFUL WHAT
YOU WISH FOR

Sometimes you have to be careful what you wish for. I had wanted to get away from Port Hedland, of course, but when I arrived back after my wonderful long weekend in Broome, I found an urgent telegram from Steve Wallace in Perth, asking if I was prepared to relieve the Jigalong headmaster, who had been hospitalised with hepatitis.

I knew little of Jigalong, other than that it was a remote Indigenous community on the edge of the Great Sandy Desert, and that quite a few of the Pindan mob were from there. Jigalong was 547 kilometres from Hedland and I was told it would take about ten and a half hours to drive that distance, along rough, sandy desert tracks. The township had originally been established in the 1900s as a location for maintenance and ration stores for workers on the rabbit-proof fence, and in 1947 a Christian mission had been established there by the Apostolic Church. Like Forrest River Mission, it also had a state school run by the Western Australian Education Department.

I was excited at the thought of going there, but Tony thought it impossible, as he had no one to relieve me at the staging school, so we sent a telegram back to that effect and I quickly came back down to earth. That night another telegram came from Perth, asking if the wife of one of the other Hedland teachers, herself a teacher, would take my class, just while I was relieving. After many refusals she finally agreed, but then we had to try to find transport to get me to Jigalong, quickly.

The Royal Flying Doctor Service was due to go out the following Tuesday as far as Nullagine, which was about halfway to Jigalong, so I sat back thinking that that would be the earliest I'd leave, at least five days away. The next day, Tony sent one of his school kids out to the shed on a bike at about 11.30 a.m., telling me that the RFDS had an emergency at Nullagine and they wanted me to go with them straight away. I told my mob to go home and stay at the camp until they were asked to come back by the new teacher.

We flew out of Hedland at 12.30 p.m. in the RFDS Cessna. I had a case full of wet and unironed clothes that I'd grabbed off the line, plus my camera, unprocessed film to take photos with, and writing paper. It happened so fast that I sat in the plane a bit stunned and bewildered, wondering what I had actually let myself in for.

I thought Nullagine was a station, but flying over it, I realised it was a small town. There was one pub, a combined post office and store, a police station with living quarters attached, a Native Hostel building, a Road Board office, a schoolhouse and hall, and two other houses besides. That made nine buildings, apart from the surrounding Aboriginal people's camps.

The countryside was very pretty. The manager of the nearby Blue Specks Mines drove me into town, and along the way we met the manager of the Native Hostel, who was driving out to meet me because he had heard on the pedal radio that I was flying in. He invited me to stay at the hostel overnight, rather than at the pub; after previous pub stays, I happily agreed. There were fifteen little boys living at the hostel, under the care of the manager and his wife; it was noisy, but fun.

The next day I watched rations being given out at the hostel and I met three mothers of my big girls at the staging school. They were all very excited when I told them about their girls and their progress at school. The manager told me a bit about the Apostolic mob running Jigalong, saying they were the ones who speak in tongues and are often moved dramatically by the Holy Spirit. This makes them sometimes faint, scream, shout or throw themselves around. I really did wonder what I had let myself in for.

I had to wait another day before travelling out to Jigalong. The school inspector, Mr Bainbridge, and an itinerant teacher, whom I'd seen and farewelled in Hedland after they'd inspected the staging school before Easter, were continuing their inspections around the state. Their trip across the nor'west was slow, because of the vast distances, and stopping at every school for inspections along the way. Having inspected Marble Bar School, they had now reached Nullagine; they got quite a shock to see me there, until I explained about the RFDS emergency and the situation at Jigalong.

We set off the next morning, after they had finished inspecting the local school, passing a lot of empty bogged vehicles between Nullagine and Jigalong, and were very lucky to get through ourselves. The itinerant teacher had a Willys Jeep, which seemed to be able to go anywhere.

We arrived in Jigalong and I was met by the principal's wife, Dot Cruthers. It was nice to see her again; I hadn't seen her since teachers' college. She was yet another young teacher experiencing distance education, now alone, with her husband sick in hospital. She was happy to see me as well.

There seemed to be no love lost between the teachers and the missionaries. The Cruthers worked hard at the school, but made no effort to join in with any sort of mission life. To me at the time, this seemed to lessen the effectiveness of their job, but later I came to understand why. They seemed to have some of the same problems as at FRM—lack of finance to get the proposed sheep station at the mission on its feet, and a lack of trained staff.

On the mission itself, there were only dormitory kids and a few working girls living in the compound. The camp was less than a kilometre away and the kids went to and from there before and after school every day. The discipline was very lax. Stealing, fighting and destructiveness were bad. At school, a room couldn't be left unlocked for five minutes without something being taken. Dot told me the news that three of the bigger girls had run off with men the day before I arrived, and there was a bit of a stir through the camp as a result.

I started at school the next day to find that seven boys were not present, as per the roll. They turned up that night and were brought before the mission's superintendent, who made them promise before God never to do it again, before getting the cane on their bottoms. If they cried, there were more strikes from the cane. They were supposed to be whacked again at school, but I didn't want to wield the cane, so the superintendent came in and did it. This was apparently a common occurrence: the way to stop them running off was to belt them. It obviously wasn't working as a deterrent; the kids were still running away!

There was much distrust of the government at Jigalong—as much as, and possibly more than, I'd already experienced with the Pindan mob—and they had good reason. Many of the Jigalong families had experienced the forced removal of mixed-heritage children from their families. One of those taken was Molly Kelly, who, together with her younger sister Daisy and cousin Gracie, had been sent to Moore River Settlement, just north of faraway Perth, in 1931. The story of Molly's remarkable escape with Daisy and Gracie and their epic return on foot to Jigalong was told by Molly's daughter in her celebrated book *Follow the Rabbit-Proof Fence*.

As well as this, there were still families coming in to Jigalong from the Great Sandy Desert. They had limited English and little understanding of the white man's ways.

53

JIGALONG

I went to the mission church and, apart from the different type of prayers and choruses, quite enjoyed it. One night, I joined with the staff in going to the camp outside the mission to see them try to 'save a few souls'. I prayed, sang choruses and clapped along like any good Apostolic.

While we were there, there was a big noise back at the mission. The superintendent's wife left immediately to see what was wrong, and by the time we got back, she was on her knees beside a girl—praying for her. The girl was kicking around in the dirt, howling and making a dreadful din. The other missionaries joined in the noise; they were almost shouting at God to release the child from Satan's power. When the girl finally stopped crying, they praised Him for another victory over the devil. Prayer seemed to be the answer for everything.

They took the girl to their house, washed her and then took her back to the dormitory. While putting her to bed, the superintendent nearly fainted at the sight of another girl silently sobbing on one of the beds, with her face in a pool of blood. Most of one of her ears was missing! It seemed that they had been praying over the wrong girl. There had been a fight between three girls aged between thirteen and fifteen. The girl they had just brought back from the house had thrown a tea chest at another girl earlier on; during the fight, she had bitten that girl's ear off. The ear was found next morning, and the superintendent's wife pickled it. I have absolutely no idea why.

The people were all well fed. The kids ran pretty wild, leading carefree lives; they spent a lot of time out at the camp. The camp was very different from FRM in that there were mostly young people and family groups living out there. All the preschool kids still lived with their families in the camp. FRM had been going for a lot longer; Jigalong had only started as a mission after the Second World War and they were still getting people coming in out of the desert. The three girls who had been fighting were among these, having come in earlier in the year.

After I had been two weeks at Jigalong, we had reports back from Port Hedland that Rod Cruthers was steadily improving and could be back on the following Thursday's Flying Doctor visit. Whether he'd be right for work then or not we didn't know, but with the May school holidays only one week after his return, he told Dot that he could rest up for the additional two weeks before school started again. My worries were for my kids, my various jobs at Hedland and whether I'd get back in time to get to Wyndham and FRM for the May school holidays.

The Thursday arrived, but there was no Flying Doctor, nor Dot's husband. Apparently the plane had broken down at

Roebourne. We were told the next day that there would be no hope of getting him back before the coming Friday, eight days away. But I wanted to be in Wyndham that weekend to meet up with Tom.

Just jokingly, I told Dot Cruthers we could pinch her husband's car and drive to Port Hedland. She jumped at the idea. We sent him an urgent radio message asking permission. He was delighted with the idea of getting away from hospital, so we made plans to leave early Saturday morning, and they would drive back the following day for the last week of school.

At lunchtime on that Friday, a little boy broke his arm, but before setting it all the missionary staff had to stop work and pray for him. The poor little man had to wait as they prayed over him before the nurse could put his arm in a cast. Dot and I had had enough; we decided to get away after school that day, taking the boy with us to get his arm x-rayed and properly set in Port Hedland. One of the missionaries checked over the car and we left at four o'clock. I was a little bit nervous about driving on those tracks and all the creek crossings, but we made Nullagine just after ten that night, without any mishap, except hitting an owl. There were lots of them on the road, and we often had to stop for kangaroos.

We left Nullagine at 7 a.m. the next morning. Dot had a few short goes at driving, and we called in at Marble Bar for a break. Here the Native Affairs man told me that he had just finished rounding up five of my schoolboys from stations. After I'd left Hedland, three of the big boys had cleared out on a truck and got jobs at Coongan Station with some other strangers. A couple of others decided they wanted some excitement too, so they also went. One of them was still in Marble Bar. When I returned to Hedland, I spoke on the phone to this boy's father at Marble Bar. He wanted to keep his son with him at Marble Bar so he could look after him in his old age. I persuaded him to send him back after the May holidays and I would somehow get him back home for the Christmas holidays.

I was relieved to make it back to Hedland, where I took the boy with the broken arm to hospital, and Dot to see and collect her husband. If I had *had* to stay at Jigalong for a year or two, I knew I could have made a go of it, but at the time I was very glad that I didn't.

54

BACK TO FORREST RIVER

I arrived back in Hedland with only enough time to unpack, wash my clothes and repack for the flight to Wyndham. The plane was running two hours late and I had almost given up any hope of getting the holiday I had so long looked forward to. But finally the plane did arrive and we were in the air. Tom was waiting for me at Wyndham and we left for Forrest River just an hour and a half later. During my brief stop at Wyndham, I caught up with dear Robert Roberts and he nearly squashed me with his greeting hug. It was wonderful to see him again.

Our journey to the mission was on a new barge that had come into service since I was last there. It was much more comfortable than the old launch and it offered more shade, but took just as long to navigate the waterways and tides. We arrived in the dark at 6 p.m. and received a rousing welcome from all. Louisa and I had an emotional, tearful reunion and then I had great fun trying to guess all the names of the kids. Some were hardly recognisable, they had grown so much.

The mission looked wonderful—green and lush, with water in the dam and at Daddaway. Everyone looked very healthy. Old man Jilila, who used to sing in the hospital, had died two weeks before we got there; old Udibane had also died. There were only ninety-six people left on the mission and more staff than ever before, who all seemed very happy. The policy now was to retain on the mission only those adults who could be usefully employed—plus the children and old people. Most of the young ones who had left school were in Wyndham or working out on stations.

There was a good garden, an enormous domesticated goat herd, including a few milkers, and they were also milking one or two cows. The main emphasis was on cattle work and it looked feasible as a business for both the mission and its residents. The new superintendent was very pleasant, calm, sensible and willing to learn. Father Gardner had great support from the staff. Josephine and Veronica had returned to the mission after spending three years at Derby Tech and were working in the hospital, and Lovie now had two children. It was all wonderful to see.

There was a big crowd at church that Sunday night. Robert and Louisa's son played the organ by ear. Louisa was indeed the village baker, a job that suited her to the ground. Tenny had left for holidays two weeks before our arrival, so I was unable to introduce him to Tom, but Harold was back, doing funny things like carrying boxes of eggs around and letting the bottom fall out. He still had a heart of gold and the people loved him because he was kind and let anyone go into his house.

The kids asked me to show them some of the dances that the Hedland kids knew, so I set about dancing and singing one of their corroboree songs. The kids doubled up in laughter; thinking I'd put on a bad display, I sat down in embarrassment. '*Arlee*, Sister, not that stuff,' they called. 'We mean rock'n'roll, jive—you know!' They weren't so much laughing at how I danced, but at what I danced. The fact that I didn't really know any rock'n'roll or jive also amused them. They were all still avid readers of magazines and were writing fan mail to film stars in Hollywood.

The little girls took Tom and me for a walk to Daddaway and then dived for lily roots. Old Peter then took us out to the old people's camp and showed us a lot of corroboree frames made out of wood with wool wound around them for use in the dances. Mona and I had a lot of fun and we had a mock fight with a nulla nulla each. Old Mona thought it a great joke that I had returned.

When holiday time came, no one would leave the compound unless it was on a tractor with a trailer. The trailer—loaded with mattresses, tucker boxes and other modern luxuries—was a far cry from my 'bush trip' with Robert, Louisa and the dormitory kids just three years before.

Tom and I set off the next morning for a day hike. We had breakfast at Djadjamerri, morning tea at Djila and walked on past the rock paintings to Gingarlmerri for afternoon tea. The feeling of standing hand in hand with someone you love, on top of a place like Djadjamerri at sunrise, with no worries, was just wonderful. It had always been a secret ambition of mine to be able to be with someone special at Forrest River.

It was on the sand beside Camera Pool that I remember having our first romantic cuddle. In those days, it was said that girls had on their chests either watermelons, lemons or poached eggs. I considered that mine were the poached egg variety, so I was thrilled when Tom admired them and called them rosebuds.

We arrived back at the mission in the dark after having walked twenty-six kilometres. It had been well worth it. Tom told me that he hadn't seen equivalent scenery at Geikie Gorge or Wittenoom, and I was thrilled. He so obviously enjoyed Forrest River and its people that he wanted to return in his holidays, to work.

Our short visit felt like it was over almost as soon as it began, but Tom still had work to do, so we headed back to Wyndham, on the barge, on the Tuesday night. When we arrived there, we met a new staff member who was going back to the mission on the barge. She was about twenty-two, scared of frogs and couldn't stand mud. I wished her luck and meant it, because it sounded like she'd need it. It struck me that she thought she was going on a holiday or visiting as a tourist. No doubt, she'd get that squashed out of her before long.

We spent Wednesday sleeping and looking around Wyndham. The town hadn't changed one bit. We went to the pictures that night, but we both went to sleep in the middle of it. On Thursday, Tom had to go to Kununurra on business and I accompanied him. Kununurra—with its gas street lamps, solar heaters, air conditioners and modern buildings— was very flash compared to Wyndham. I watched Tom and another PWD engineer testing samples of different riverbed soils to see if they could be used in the concrete on dams in different places. It was a wonderful, interesting, though tiring, day.

The next morning, we flew around in a Cessna for two hours. Tom, through PWD, had chartered a Cessna to look for new suitable dam sites for the town, as their present dam was insufficient. We flew the length of the King River, very low, and doing many sharp twists and turns. It was terrific scenery and a very bumpy but thrilling trip. Then we circled the town before flying out to FRM for a look. We flew very low over the mission, Djadjamerri and Gingarlmerri. Although it was interesting, it seemed a bit like sacrilege; seeing it this way made everything about that beautiful place appear so small and almost insignificant. It was as if the long, prickly rough walks and the long barge trip were being mocked from the air.

For the rest of the day Tom had to work, so I relaxed in preparation for the start of next term. Kununurra is on the Ord River, and we took tea out there before I flew back to Wyndham, and then on to Port Hedland. It looked as though Tom would be there on the new dam project for weeks.

It was a mighty holiday and something I'll never forget. Everything was perfect, and Tom and I wanted to see a lot more of each other.

Tom was still technically based in Broome, but on spare weekends he would get into his trusty VW Beetle and drive down mostly ungraded dirt roads to Hedland to see me—a round trip of almost 1300 kilometres. How that little car survived those roads is nothing short of a miracle, but survive it did!

55

MILI MILI

The start of a new term meant a move into our new school-room. It was a big day in all our lives. After watching the building of the new classrooms for nearly a year, we were ready to move in. On the first day there, one little kid was too scared at first and stood crying at the gate. He wanted to go back to the camp, but he eventually came in, his eyes as big as saucers.

That afternoon all the kids from the main school and all the parents, including those from the camp, came for the official opening, all curious to look at the new classrooms. It really was a grand building compared to the old shed. We were all completely lost and dazed. It was made of cement bricks, it had rubber tiles on cement floors, a cool under-croft, showers, push-button toilets, cold-water machines, fans, lights—everything! My class had one room and Brian Hassell's class, which had been in the town hall, had the other room. The remainder of the state school was still in the town. The new building looked out to sea over the sandhills on the town side, and we could also see the Loco Shed in the distance.

Being in a modern building and mixing with the kids from the other class made a big difference to the staging school. We had had the enormous old railway shed from September 1959 to May 1961; while it had served its purpose well, and it was exciting when a train came into the classroom, it had been a challenge to make everything into the best learning situation. We were very grateful for having had the use of the shed, but it was good to be in a proper classroom before a large number of our older kids left at the end of that year.

A lot of the thrill and glory of the move was taken away by a few white parents and their dreadful gossip. I lost friendships with the white people who started most of the rumours. They were fundamentally station people, those impacted by the strike by the Aboriginal workers, so I couldn't expect much more.

These were some of the rumours: all my girls were pregnant; my big kids were 'carrying on with each other' before I got to school in the morning; the girls all got around with their breasts hanging out; the big boys were very rough; they all had ringworm, lice, VD and so on. They were saying that the big boys were fighting the little boys and molesting the little girls, and they were asking why we were hurrying along the sex education of seven-, eight- and nine-year-olds by letting them see married women with babies at school. They said they were going to send their children to the convent or boarding schools rather than have them mix with my big boys.

A few of the big girls were now married to older men. I had to guarantee that no obviously pregnant girl would be allowed to attend school. The funniest part was that the worst complainers were those who had just had babies themselves. Phillip was still coming to school with his mum, Daisy, under protest from those same whites. We had a fairly tense meeting about that with all the white parents concerned, and it gave me indigestion for three days.

I wrote to Steve Wallace, asking about the official rules on married women being allowed to bring babies to school. There was no definite rule, and in reply he expressed the view that the sympathy of both him and Mr Thornbury, the superintendent, was with me. Their official view was that babies should not come to school; however, unofficially, he said that we could do as much as we could get away with, so long as it did not create too much protest. Thankfully, after that horrid meeting, nothing more was said; the gossip seemed to die down.

Harold Holt, who was then the federal treasurer, and Senator Spooner, who was minister for National Development, were on a nine-day tour of Western Australia and the Northern Territory, and later that week they came with their wives to Port Hedland for a day. Both Mrs Holt and Mrs Spooner visited our new school while their husbands were busy elsewhere; the two wives spent nearly all their time in Port Hedland with my class. I knew they were important people, but I tried to act normally. They adored baby Phillip, and Mrs Holt said she loved the cotton blanket his mum, Daisy, had sewn for him. When they eventually left, they took some of the kids' paintings with them as gifts; much to the kids' delight, they left one pound for them all so they could buy lollies.

~

My kids had learnt so much, both academically and socially, since we started the staging school. The big kids would help the little ones get ready for school; the boys would chop wood and collect water for the camp; the girls would mend clothes for everyone. They all took a real pride in their appearance.

For Arbor Day, we planted trees around the new classroom. After that, if anyone played up, their punishment was to carry sand and manure onto the new garden beds and water the trees or collect tins of buffel grass seed to sell. The punishment side of this failed, because they all wanted to do it!

Night school had also now moved to the new classroom, a big change from the vast and dimly lit Loco Shed. With a maximum of fifteen people, we studied literacy; some of the women continued sewing new clothing and mending old, and the men did woodwork. Most classes were at full capacity.

A Federal Parliamentary Select Committee on Aboriginal Voting Rights was touring the country, interviewing Aborigines and Torres Strait Islander peoples and whites regarding the rights of Aboriginal and Torres Straits Islander peoples to vote. But when they came to visit us, only nine adult students turned up. Everybody was very scared—they wanted me to hide them in the cupboard or throw them out the window!

The sight of about fifteen tall men in dark suits and ties was rather unnerving, even for me. They walked around, asking questions such as 'When are you going to start another class?' I didn't know any of the committee members, but two said something to me about carrying on the good work of my father. Dad had been continually making waves in Perth and the eastern states with his work as the chair of Native Welfare.

I no sooner got through shaking hands with each in turn and saying, 'Good evening,' than it felt like we had to repeat the process and say, 'Goodnight and thank you.' We gave them copies of the Pindan *Mili Mili*, with its news on both the staging and night school. Mum had been able to find a second-hand typewriter for forty pounds for me to type up the *Mili Mili*. As with most things that weren't donated and which they found for me, I sent them a cheque back to cover the costs and freight. I don't know what I would have done without my parents' wonderful support.

The following day, the committee went to the courthouse to hear submissions. Peter and Ernie spoke, and someone told me later that Peter said he didn't know what voting meant. The explanation was something like, 'Voting for the man we want to make our laws in parliament,' and he replied that that seemed too simple for all the fuss that was being made about it.

In the social studies test later that week, I asked the kids what went on in parliament. One replied, 'A big fight!' and it dawned on me that I had often spoken about people fighting for their rights in parliament. But the others laughed really loudly when he said this, and that at least showed me that thankfully they didn't all picture Parliament House as a big boxing ring.

The new classroom was getting plenty of visitors. We had a visit to night school from a young man by the name of Charlie Perkins, who would go on to become the first recognised Australian Aboriginal person to complete a university degree. He was living in South Australia at this time and was already a well-known Indigenous activist and leader. He was seeking signatures for a petition in support of state MP Don Dunstan, who was planning to introduce a private members bill to the South Australian parliament. The bill was to remove any legal restrictions on Aboriginal people. Unfortunately we only had six students turn up that night, but it was a pleasure for us all to meet Charlie Perkins and show him what we were doing.

56

MISUNDERSTANDINGS

Tom was now officially the Public Works Department assistant district engineer for the Derby district and we were corresponding regularly when he was away on the Ord River with work. His engineering job was keeping him busy and was involving him in a lot of interesting work. We were both very busy with our work, but we kept in regular contact.

Through our correspondence we learnt that we knew many of the same people. Perth was like a big country town back then. One of his Perth friends had been at uni with me and was friends with both Mick Stow and many of my uni pals, and yet we hadn't met. Mick was now back in Perth after spending a year in England.

I had spent my first year of tertiary education at the University of Western Australia, boarding at St Catherine's College. I was so immature that I'd never seen people drinking or swearing before. I was shy and awkward and had felt very isolated. I had been studying to be a high school teacher, majoring in the subjects I loved, science and maths, but I failed miserably in the exams at the end of my first year. That had been a blessing really, because I loved teachers' college and teaching the younger years.

Letters to and from Tom helped me whenever I had problems; he was a remote sounding board for everything, good and bad, that was happening in Hedland. Our relationship was going well—until my warped sense of humour came into play.

He had made disparaging comments, half in jest, about the Welsh—the proud nationality of my mother and my grandmother, whom I loved dearly—so I decided to tell him off via a letter, in what I thought was a similar tone of jest. I made derogatory comments about his German heritage, the language, and the hoicking and spitting that accompanied it. I meant it to be so outrageous that it wouldn't be believable, but, of course, when you write something, the humour doesn't necessarily come through. He didn't find a hint of love in my letter and returned it with a very short note saying, 'Thank you, it's all over.' That was it. Disaster!

I had to write back to him immediately, explaining that it was all a joke. There then followed a few miserable days while I waited for the postal service to bring me a message, hopefully of forgiveness. It arrived at last, but I didn't have a clean slate yet.

~

The inter school athletics championships were on again in June, this time in Port Hedland, with the Wittenoom and Marble Bar kids travelling to us. We had eighteen gym tunics and bloomers to make for the girls, and we needed to sew blue stripes on nineteen pairs of white shorts for the boys. The big girls and I were busy—our kids were going to look wonderful, all thirty-seven of them.

With me helping with the sports clothes, the little kids were left to go wild, playing 'chuckin'' games with plasticine. They'd all certainly come out of their nervous shells, like jets, since moving into the new classroom, and were all speaking and pronouncing English much better. The big boys were having hairdressing lessons from a barber in town and had been writing up notes on the uses of carpentry tools, which had finally arrived from Perth. Everyone had made an impressive improvement both academically and practically, being in the new school.

MMA asked the Two Mile mob, through me, if they would be willing to put on a dance display for tourists. I requested that the dancers be paid. Peter asked the mob and it was decided that the night before the upcoming Port Hedland horse races later in August could work, as there would be plenty of the Pindan mob in town and there was sure to be a corroboree anyway. I sent a message back to MMA, confirming that the night would be in a couple of months' time.

In the midst of all this, we received notice that a children's fancy dress party—one of those delightful events that used to be held back then—was going to be on the following weekend. My kids got the message the same as everyone else did, but I had so much on my hands with the sports uniform sewing that I did nothing to encourage them. However, on the Friday, I heard that one of the organising ladies had said that it would be better if my kids didn't go. That did it—it was a red rag to a bull. The big boys went as corroboree men, and one of them even received a prize; the girls dressed up as their favourite characters. It was good to see everyone enjoying themselves so much.

At the nasty parents' meeting sometime previously, one or two of the white parents had expressed their concerns about mixing my class with the other class. One of the parents who had been most worried at the time ended up apologising to me at the fancy dress party, saying he was sorry he had listened to the rumours. At the end of the evening, the 'lady' who had apparently made the comment about it being best if my kids didn't attend melted before the night was out and gave me all the leftovers from the supper for 'my people'.

It was at about this time that my big brother, John, visited me again, on his way back to Indonesia. He came to the school and talked to my kids about the *wayang* shadow puppet theatre performances he had seen in Indonesia, then he had a lot of fun trying to learn how to throw a boomerang. These were not carved wooden ones, like the cultural bush type; these were made out of the metal strapping that came around wooden crates. The big boys would cut off about 45 centimetres and fold it at right angles in the middle. I think they were called 'kylies', and they were lethal to birds or other game.

John wrote home, 'Lined up to march into school in the morning, the classes looked keen and it was good to think the kids were getting a chance to learn the skills they would need in their new lives in a whole new society.' I agreed. That is what I loved about the staging school: it gave them an opportunity to further their white-man education, academically and practically, while still retaining their culture.

That week the town had a visiting Wild West show arrive and there was much excitement. The performance was in the town hall with Colt 45s, stockwhip displays and country songs accompanied by guitars. The white population was offered chairs, but almost the entire native population of Hedland happily paid twelve shillings each, and six shillings for each child, to stand or sit on tables around the walls. There were also plenty of people outside, peeking through the shutters, trying to see the show. An enjoyable night, despite the discrimination.

57

RACES AND
MERRY-GO-ROUNDS

The annual round of horse racing was almost on us and Ernie had the same concerns he always faced at this time, the impact that an increase in visitors and the flow of alcohol would have on the camp.

School attendance hadn't been nearly as good since we moved out of the shed. The kids would stay away for any little reason they could find. Mr Bainbridge was due again, so any leisure time came to a sudden halt as I made sure all the school bookwork was up to date. I did worry that my students wouldn't all be there—two of the older girls were pregnant, and one of the boys had taken a job on a station.

No one turned up to night school on the first evening that the merry-go-round started up in town, and I held real concern for the promised MMA corroboree. Peter told me that it would be all right, but it turned out that the attraction of the merry-go-round and the other sideshow stalls was simply too great. A small number of adults and most of my kids ended up doing some dances for just five female tourists.

One dance I found funny: it depicted two drunks being arrested by a sergeant.

The tourists didn't seem to be the type who would appreciate a good corroboree, so I wasn't worried about the small repertoire. Peter, though, was very disappointed with his mob and told me he thought there would be a lot of race visitors in gaol before the weekend was over.

The pattern was virtually the same as the previous year. Once again a number of the things Ernie was worried about took place, leading to yet another punishment session. As before, few of my kids attended classes on the Monday, so I went out to the camp to find out who would be coming to my night class. As previously, alcohol was again involved, and there was concern that some boys, who weren't classified as 'proper' men by the mob, were chasing girls without regard to skin relationships.

Peter Coffin came to the school a few weeks later, to tell me that they were taking all the kids to a *Bukli* meeting at Twelve Mile in two weeks' time; he invited me to attend. At a *Bukli* meeting, young men are welcomed back to their mob after having been in the bush with Elders for about six weeks. During that time they went through the process of being made a 'proper man', which included being taught about their responsibilities, the law and hunting methods.

Having witnessed a *Bukli* meeting previously, I wasn't sure I needed to attend another one, but I knew it was important, and a privilege to be asked. I agreed to go and asked if Tom, who was driving down from Broome, could also attend.

58

BUKLI MEETING

On the day of the *Bukli* meeting, most of the kids from the One Mile and Two Mile were taken by truck straight after lunch to Kedjerina, about twenty-six kilometres from the town. Tom and I followed at 4 p.m., after Tom had just driven the more than six hundred kilometres from Broome. I met him at the turn-off from the main highway and told him what was going to happen. He said, 'Look I've just driven all this way to see you. Can't we go into town?'

I told him, 'The women won't have any tops on.' We went.

We were a little late for the initial meeting, but as I had seen one before, I didn't think we were in for much. I was certainly proven wrong.

A group of people were camped at Kedjerina permanently. There were little humpies dotted around, surrounded by dogs, billies and burnt-out fires. Little kids romped around in the sand, just like any kids let loose on a wide lawn or beach. They weren't very interested in what the adults were doing.

The *Bukli*—meaning, one of the young men learning the law—was danced along the wide, dry riverbed by all his distant relations to the meeting spot, where his close relatives were sitting in a large group, wailing. As the *Bukli* came into sight, the wailing became louder and some of the women, who were sitting separately from the men, became hysterical. They hit themselves with fists or old tins, and sometimes jumped up screaming. There were a few older women standing behind them, to control their outbursts so no one was hurt. At this meeting there were two *Bukli*; each of them had a very tight string tied around the top of their arm, which was left there until the rest of their arm swelled up and felt numb. This was happening while the *Bukli* watched the dance. The two family groups—all the relations (on the father's and mother's side, I presumed)—stamped around in circles, trying to hit each other with branches and throw water over each other, all in fun. In front of them were many bags of flour, packets of tea and other presents of food for the distant relatives. This ensured that they would have enough tucker for their stay and their return trip.

The escorts handed their *Bukli* over and then retired in a group while he was being met by his close relations. 'Being met' consisted of being helped down to, and then up from, the knees of the relatives. Their emotions reached fever pitch and died down as he passed on to the next one. This was the stage at which Tom and I arrived.

The distant relatives were mainly from Nullagine and Jigalong, and the close ones from around Hedland. This was the biggest Pindan gathering any of my school children had been at and I estimated there were between a hundred and fifty and two hundred people present. The Jigalong mob were brightly decorated with bands of red wool around their upper arms and foreheads, while white, fluffy-looking pairs of sticks, like horns, were fixed to a band around their heads. Their chests and backs were smeared with red ochre, with drops and patterns in white ochre or feathers. Most of the men wore shorts and the women wore skirts; all tops were bare. The Hedland mob had blackened their backs and chests and had different coloured bands around their arms and foreheads. In some armbands, there were bunches of shaved wood and fluffy feathers. All men wore their *djineen* (a flat stick pointed at both ends and carved) across the back of their heads. The men in the front row of the close relatives held brightly coloured shields. Most men of both groups carried at least one boomerang and maybe a shield and/or spear and a woomera.

All the children and visitors who were not directly concerned with the corroboree were standing or sitting nearby in groups. The only white people present were Jim Hallum, who I think may have been from Native Affairs; a man called Frank, who was employed by Pindan; and Tom and me. My big boys just looked like any gang of teenagers watching a passing parade. They were dressed in their school clothes, with the addition of a cap or old fishing hat and a rolled-up comic book sticking out of a back pocket.

At this meeting, one of the *Bukli* was Dalgety, one of my first enrolments at the school two years ago. He would have been about twenty then. He had been taken all the way to Jigalong. From there the group of distant relatives took him back to Moolyella (Marble Bar) and then refused to come any further. They thought that was where the meeting should have been held, but I never knew why. The Port Hedland mob argued that the meeting should be held at Kedjerina because that was where Dalgety's parents were. For two weeks the Jigalong mob camped at Moolyella until the Hedland mob asked Native Affairs to persuade them to come in. Peter Coffin told me later that if they had all gone to Moolyella, there would have been a really big fight.

After Dalgety had been met by all his relatives, and the wailing had stopped, about five Jigalong men ran out and stood in a row about thirty metres away from the other group. They held boomerangs or spears and shields and were shouting something that we couldn't understand. The Hedland mob shouted back, but Peter Coffin, Ernie Mitchell and a few others waved them back and tried to quieten everyone down.

I thought it was all just a bit of fun, but one man came and told us we had better step back as this was developing into a genuine fight. A kindly looking man with a *wokaburra* (a fighting stick) stood beside us and I asked him if this confrontation was dinkum. He laughed and said, 'No, only play.' He must have been trying to stop me from getting frightened.

The *Buklis* were required to just sit and watch, which they did as the tension unfolded. Again, some of the visiting warriors faced the others. A few people on both sides started to look angry. Men shouted and waved boomerangs or spears and women struggled with them, trying to take their weapons away. A few started running towards the opposite side and finally someone—I don't remember from which side—let fly with a boomerang. That started it. Boomerangs started whizzing to and from each side, mainly along the ground but at least one went high up and returned. Most of the women were well into it as well, struggling to get the boomerangs from their men folk.

Up till then, we had been standing fairly close, but when I saw my schoolboys run, I followed them to get behind a truck. I was a bit scared and I shouted out to Tom to take shelter too, but he was too busy taking photos!

One of the Hedland men, Teddy Allen, had his leg badly cut by a boomerang. It had cut through his long jeans like a knife. His injury narrowed the fight down to himself and the man whose boomerang had hit him. All the others were either trying to help or stop these two. After a lot of scuffling, which I couldn't sort out, they forced Teddy back into his place and made signs that the fight had finished.

A group of about five old women wobbled and shook around Teddy as they cried in sympathy for him. Peter Coffin told us he had tried to stop these women because all their 'goings on' made the man feel sorry for himself and more determined to get even.

Once or twice, Teddy tried to jump up and run towards the other mob, but he was successfully held down until finally he made a getaway. His opponent was just as eager to collect punishment as Teddy was to give it, and people were trying to restrain him from running across to collect it. When they came together, Teddy gave him some mighty hard cracks with a shield, but he still didn't seem satisfied. I was told later that this was because he hadn't drawn blood.

Teddy tried to grab spears from the other men and finally he got one. In a blind rage he ran up to his enemy, who stood his ground, turned sideways and planted his foot in the ground with his leg stiff and straight. Teddy thrust the spear right through his opponent's leg so that it protruded out the other side of his thigh and then he withdrew it.

There was wailing everywhere, but the fighting was over and the scattered spectators started to gather again. At this point I felt sick and wanted to go home. Tom didn't seem anxious to go, so we stayed, and the ceremony continued.

Teddy and his opponent hugged each other and had a good old cry; they even shook hands. They would be friends for life. During the night, whenever they met, they would begin the hugging and crying all over again. Neither appeared to be limping, nor had they treated their wounds.

It was now time for the presents to be given out. The Jigalong crowd all assembled ready to dance toward the presents. Some of the Hedland men called for me to come closer to get a better photo. No longer scared, Tom and I both moved in. There was some very lively dancing with high knee stamping. Ernie Mitchell led the Hedland mob and really surprised me with his agility, considering his age and paunch. The flour and tea took about half an hour to distribute to the right people. Then there was just a finish-off dance and an hour's break for tea.

Everyone joined their family group and lit campfires. We saw Peter Coffin showing Teddy how he should have used his shield to protect himself from the boomerang.

Sitting back at our own campfire, I shared with Tom what I'd seen in the middle of the fight: a delightful pair of old men, one of them wearing baggy pants tied with string, a narrow-brimmed hat pulled down tightly on his forehead and a mug tied on one hip. His shirt was old and checked and he carried a waterbag. The other was one of the ceremony men; he had very little paint, but bright blue woollen bands around his arms and forehead. The two of them took no notice of the fight; they came up and hugged each other and quietly sobbed together as if it had been a long time since they had last met. After about ten minutes of this, they turned their backs on the others and started chatting away like any two men on a street corner.

After boiling our billy and making tea, Tom and I were lying by our campfire when we noticed a satellite slowly travelling across the sky. It seemed most incongruous, and I pointed it out to the group nearest us. They showed scant regard and said, 'Oh yes, I see 'im,' then laughed and went on with their conversation.

After tea, the dance that followed was one that had come from Roebourne; it was one that the visiting mob wished to see. The dancing was done by the women, while the men sat in the middle singing and banging their shields in such a way that it made a resounding hollow thud. The women shuffled in a perfect circle around the men, digging a furrow as they went. Each little section of the dance was finished by the women giving a little shout and waving a twig of leaves or their hands towards the centre.

While the dancing was going on, three or four men grabbed all the brothers, uncles and cousins of the *Bukli* one by one and laid them on the ground. An older woman then had to find each man's wife, or a woman who was the right skin name to be his wife. The wife—or woman of the right skin—then had to lie on top of the man, kiss him and then help him up and brush his back. This part was all just good fun. We were sitting near some of my schoolgirls who were married. They pretended to be nervous and coy, and giggled when they had to go up to lie on top of their husband. When we left at 10.30 p.m. this was still going on. We passed Peter and his wife Biddy Coffin. Peter was exhausted and had no voice left. We gave some people a lift back to town, but most stayed on for the whole weekend.

After the evening's entertainment, which was helped along by a few *mumias* or clowns, the *Buklis* are taken back into the bush for another two weeks. Then they are free to carry on with their normal lives.

Teddy Allen was a well-respected man with a job in town. He just wore jeans and a T-shirt, and wasn't decorated like the others. However, he took part in everything and seemed most upset about the Jigalong mob refusing to come in to Kedjerina. The man he had speared was his cousin. I was concerned that their wounds hadn't been treated, but the kids told me that the two injured men would probably pour kerosene and rub ash over their wounds to stop any infection.

The next day at school, I asked the kids to draw what they'd seen. I still have and cherish some of the most incredible pictures they drew. It truly was a memorable day for everyone who had been there.

59

AN UNLIKELY PROPOSAL

Family news via the mail was always a joy to receive. My brother Bob, now an architect, had announced his engagement to a lovely nurse, Kate. Anne and Adrian had a daughter, Sandra; John was still in Indonesia, married to a lovely Italian lady, Victoria; and Susie was in her last years of high school, trying to study through all the family excitement. Mum and Dad were still heavily involved with Allawah Grove, the Native Welfare Council, the United Nations and Quakers. Our family lives were full.

Tom was back in Broome and he came down to Hedland whenever he could. It took nine hours each way to drive the more than six hundred kilometres, leaving us little time together. I spent a week of my September school holidays in Broome with him and caught up with Bishop one night and Dad's boss, Horrie Miller, who had a holiday house there. A wonderful break away.

In early October, I received a letter from Tom asking me to marry him. I must admit it was not the romantic down-on-one-knee-with-ring-in-hand kind of proposal that most women imagine, but it was a wonderful letter nonetheless. I guess he had finally forgiven me for my mocking German references. We had talked about marriage before, but a major drawback was that the Education Department generally barred married women from teaching. I'd have to resign. Essentially, it was a toss-up between the two loves of my life—teaching and Tom—and Tom won.

He waited for my written reply, and then drove down that weekend. I was so happy. I wrote to all the jewellers in the phone book, asking them to send catalogues, and we spent all of the next Saturday choosing an engagement ring and sending off the order.

We wanted to wait until we met our respective parents before making the announcement public, but our secret snuck out anyway. It was probably my happy glow as I went about my day that gave it away. Tom told Bishop and he gave us our first wedding present—three pewter, glass-bottomed mugs which he had won at deck quoits on the *Koolama* in his early days in the North West. He wrote to me to express his congratulations and said that nothing would make him happier than marrying us. I corresponded with Tom's family, and his mum met my family in Perth before I could get there. She wrote after the visit, thanking me for introducing her to the happy Gare family, and my heart soared. I really wanted to be back in Perth with all of these people, but I would have to wait.

We held an engagement party at the home of the Glasses, with Tony Barker and Mr Bainbridge among the guests. We made the announcement in front of all our Hedland friends and then the long-awaited ring was planted on my finger.

I put in my resignation for the end of the school year, and we planned to marry in March the following year. I resigned from usheretting at the pictures and night school had finished up because most of the Pindan mob were out working. This gave me more time at home during the week to catch up with everything so I could spend more time with Tom when he came down. I still had Cubs, Guides, which had started that year, and church duties, but, as the weather started to become more humid, basketball and tennis matches petered out. I felt like I had so much time and I busied myself making quite a few knickknacks for my glory box, but I started to run out of ideas for things that could be made with the limited material available. Once again Mum came to the rescue and sent me up yet more material and thread.

I was really happy with how my students were going. A large number of the older kids would be leaving at the end of the year, and the younger ones were now a part of the school, having caught up to the academic level of the white kids. The staging school had been a success. What had started in the incredible old train shed had worked, not only for the kids, but for a lot of the adults at Two Mile as well. They could now read and write, some in a rather rudimentary fashion, and had work and life skills that would help them get employment.

Tony informed me that they were planning on starting a junior high school in Port Hedland the following year, for about twenty-five kids from Port Hedland, Marble Bar, Jigalong, Nullagine, Wittenoom and possibly Roebourne. Many of the out-of-town kids would be boarding in private homes. An exciting time for the town and I was a little sad that I wouldn't see it.

We found out that Tom would be stationed at Wyndham the following year, and that the Public Works Department would be building us a new home. I was excited at the prospect in so many ways, as I knew Wyndham and its people well.

Tom now came down each weekend and helped me sort out all the school bits and pieces. For the last few weeks of term the whole of our precious day together was spent at the school, and we even had all our meals out there. Tom cleaned and serviced my scooter. We decided to keep it because it was in such good working condition, even though its outside paint was wearing off and its appearance was not terribly good. Also no one would want to buy a second-hand scooter so, even if it was undignified at the time for a married woman to ride a scooter, we kept it.

I packed up all my belongings and said 'Goodbye'. It was a long, sad process. I was happy going into my new role as a wife, and hopefully a mother, who would still be living and working in the North West, but saying goodbye to my Hedland family, both Aboriginal and non-Aboriginal, wrenched at my heart.

In among it all, I received a letter from Mick Stow, congratulating me on my upcoming marriage. He was heading off to England to become a lecturer at a university in Leeds, and I was really pleased for him.

60

BISHOP

I arrived back in Perth just before Christmas and spent the next two months organising our wedding for 3 March. I set about making my own wedding dress and a dress for Susie, who would be my bridesmaid, and a beautiful, and of course practical, going-away outfit. First a lightweight reversible coat, which was olive green on the outside and lined with a deep bluish-grey floral material. I made a straight dress out of the olive material with a hat to match and a full-skirted dress out of the floral material. This meant many options for later use. Dad was disappointed that I hadn't made a long-skirted wedding dress, but I thought a short one would be more useful afterwards, even if I was heading back up to the red soils of the Kimberley, and the dress was white.

Tom had always imagined himself being married in the chapel at Guildford Grammar, and I had always imagined a Quaker wedding in the Darlington hills among the wildflowers. Dear little St Cuthbert's in Darlington was to be a very happy compromise. I still love that little church.

Bishop Frewer had already agreed to officiate at our wedding, which ended up being a bit of a coup because one of his clergy was also getting married on the same day at Mt Magnet and had also asked him to officiate on that same weekend. Bishop opted to come to Darlington and be with us.

The 3rd of March was a boiling hot day, and I remember me in my petticoat running around Mum and Dad's backyard, where the reception was to be held, hurriedly putting out place cards on tables for all the guests. We arrived at the church, Dad proudly holding on to my arm, and the local reverend in a bit of a fluster because a real-live bishop was in his parish!

The choirmaster at Guildford Grammar was there to play the organ as we entered the church and throughout the ceremony. Mum sang a solo, making our family emotional. Bishop conducted the service beautifully, but to my embarrassment paid tribute to my teaching work up in the North West, as Tom beamed at me proudly.

As we walked out of the church, we had an unofficial guard of honour from six of my former pupils, each wearing their shy smiles and a pink floral wreath around their hair. The North West Camp School was on, and one of the teachers had organised for them to attend—three girls from Port Hedland and three from Forrest River. Bishop beamed, as they were some of his flock from the furthest reaches of his diocese. We felt so privileged to have them all involved on our special day.

Dad's brother drove us off into the bush for wedding photos while the guests went to Mum and Dad's. My hurried place-name distribution had all been for naught because, by the time we returned, the cards were all over the place, blown about by the hot afternoon breeze.

At about 9 p.m. we departed, in Tom's trusty VW Beetle. When Tom and his best man, an old school friend, had been driving to the wedding that morning they had stopped at the brand new Boomerang Hotel on the Albany Highway to drop Tom's luggage, thinking a room had been booked previously. However, the office staff had mislaid the booking and there were no vacancies. They had managed to ring the Mundaring Weir Hotel and book us in there.

It was pretty comical—Tom and I in our smart going-away outfits arriving late at night at this adorable little two-storey wooden pub set in the bush. We walked in to find a group of people singing 'Clementine' around an old piano. They gave us their best room for the night.

We were served breakfast in bed the next morning. After that, we strolled around the garden and down to the dam site, before packing and driving back to Darlington to pick up our luggage. Then it was on to the airport for our honeymoon— in Tom's old hometown, Bangkok.

61

INTEGRATION

To both our surprise and delight, we returned to Australia from our six-week Thailand honeymoon to find I was pregnant. John was born in Wyndham in December 1962.

We stayed in the North West for many years, moving from town to town on different engineering projects with Tom's work. John was followed seventeen months later by the arrival of our beautiful daughter, Wendy, then our second son, Andrew, arrived three years after that. I spent all of that time raising our little family in often primitive conditions, and I relished the challenge.

Then in 1971 I started relief teaching at a little two-roomed private school, Helena School in Darlington. At the end of 1972, we bought a block with a classroom from the two elderly ladies who owned the school, and I became not only a married teacher, but the female principal of a school that was inclusive of all people. I tried to retire three times over the years but was always pulled back. I loved to teach and would at any opportunity. Currently, at the age of eighty-six, I help convene Alternative to Violence Project (AVP) workshops in Western Australian and Northern Territory communities, prisons and schools. But that is a whole other story!

~

I look back at the years described in this narrative with a mixture of emotions. I am forever grateful that my wonderful mother kept all of my letters; reading back through them, memories of times forgotten and wonderful people have flooded back.

With its two distinct seasons, the Wet and the Dry, Forrest River had the beauty of a real-life Eden. A place of abundance and beauty, where tucker was plentiful and the scenery breathtaking. But, like that biblical place, it could be a paradise easily spoiled by people's behaviour and actions. I truly think that more good than bad happened at the Forrest River Mission, though my letters home were full of dealing with difficult relationships and the resulting conflicts between the white staff. Fresh from college and leaving my family home for the first time, perhaps this was more a sign of how young and inexperienced I was about the world and its people.

I know that the medical care and food available at Forrest River certainly kept many Oombulgurri alive, though I sometimes wonder if the mission made it all too easy for a people who were used to taking what they needed from the land when they needed it.

Many Aboriginal people have been kicked off living on their own Country as it has been taken up by agriculture, and later mining. It was against the law to trespass—that was the white man's law. The Oombulgurri were fortunate, I think, that they could still go out on their Country, and this kept a lot of their traditions and culture alive, even in the mission. But, with food available through the store, there was no daily need to go out and hunt. When it came to some of the Pindan mob, coming in from the harsh desert country and discovering readily available food must have provided a great impetus for them to leave their old life behind.

At Forrest River, I witnessed the problems of trying to integrate Aboriginal people into white society—to introduce the concept of wages and an understanding of the value of money. Problem gambling became a serious issue. Problems were also starting to emerge with the availability of tobacco and sugar in their diet, and of alcohol introduced through unscrupulous white men in town.

My father had always believed that having Aboriginal people integrate into society, rather than assimilate, was the better way forward. To assimilate is to wholly adopt the ways of another culture and to fully become a part of a different society, whereas to integrate allows individuals from different groups to incorporate into a society as equals. Equality and respect have to be shown by both sides for integration to work successfully. This was something my parents instilled in us from an early age and worked tirelessly on in their work with Quakers, the Native Welfare Council and the United Nations.

Seeing the missions at Yarrabah and Jigalong was a contrast to what I had experienced at Forrest River in several ways, even though I was only in both places for a short time. Every mission throughout the north was different—some encouraged culture, others didn't.

Seeing the dormitory kids at Forrest River was the first time I had experienced kids being brought into some sort of pastoral care. At that time, many whites believed it was right to take the children because the standard of living in the mob was not up to the white man's standard. We judged by our standards, not theirs. Going camping with Robert and Louisa and the dormitory kids showed me how well they could live in their traditional ways. They (and I, while I was with them) may have been filthy dirty by white man standards, but they were happy and healthy.

When Tom and I visited Forrest River again in 1960, it was a delight to see the mission being run by plenty of staff; the inhabitants were happy and occupied in helping the place grow. But the mission was closed in 1969, after the 1967 Aboriginal citizenship referendum.

During our two years in Wyndham after we were married, I would regularly catch up and have visits from Oombulgurri living both in the town and out at the mission. Bishop Frewer continued to be a regular visitor also. He and Tom would build and open the humble little St Boniface church in 1962, the first Anglican church in Wyndham. Bishop finally retired to Perth in 1965 after being the Bishop of North West Australia since 1928.

I have been lucky enough to connect with some of my old students and their families. Una Millard's granddaughter, Madison, came to visit recently, and we were having a discussion about her starting up a bush tucker business. She doesn't like that most Aboriginal businesses seem to be run by white fellas and she wants to set up her own. My son John offered to help her create a business plan, and I love that he could help Una's granddaughter. The link between FRM in the 1950s and modern times is wonderful. Una had been one of my older Girl Guides, and a great help with the little ones.

Another Girl Guide from FRM I've also managed to contact is Suzy Anderson. Suzy had been one of the two girls to visit Perth when Lady Baden-Powell was there. The girls had stayed with my parents; when I asked her about the trip, the only thing Suzy could remember was when she and my youngest sister were chased by a dog while walking through Darlington! That did make me laugh. She still has lovely memories of some of the things we used to do in Girl Guides at Forrest River, which lightens my heart.

In 2017 I was helping run community AVP workshops in Port Hedland for the Bloodwood Tree Association, a not-for-profit organisation providing services and support to at-risk Aboriginal and Torres Strait Islander people. A couple of doors down from the Bloodwood Tree building is a Pilbara Aboriginal Language Centre; I'd been told they had old photos of Port Hedland displayed that I might be interested in looking at, so I went for a walk to find a local being interviewed by an Australian Institute of Aboriginal and Torres Strait Islander Studies researcher about Indigenous language. They were talking about the railway line and the researcher was very excited when I showed her some of my old Loco Shed photos. The next time I went to Hedland to do workshops, the researcher organised a reunion and asked me to give a presentation of my time in Port Hedland with the school.

It was wonderful to see some of my ex-students, both of the Loco Shed school and the night school, including Daisy Tinker and Nyaparu (William) Gardner. Tommy Gardner, our Wittenoom athletics champion, was in the hospital, so he couldn't make the trip for the reunion. It was sad to hear of those who had already passed on. Many of the children and grandchildren of some of my students were fascinated by the old stories and photographs. We spent a lot of time putting names to photos and talking about the school days. It was incredible to hear their memories of that time and place.

The other speaker that day was Kevin Allen, the son of Teddy Allen, whom Tom and I had witnessed being hit by the boomerang at the *Bukli* meeting all those years ago. Kevin was born after the *Bukli* meeting; he had seen the scar on his father's leg, and knew how he got it, but his dad hadn't talked about the event with him. Kevin lives in Perth, and we met up in Midland before the Port Hedland 2018 reunion. I showed him the photos and drawings the kids had done after the meeting. He kept shaking his head and saying, 'You were there?' Of course, in 2018 I was an old grey-haired woman, not the skinny white girl in the photos.

Kevin now works in royalties and land rights for the Njamal Trust, and he and his wife agreed to come and talk with the Aboriginal studies kids at Helena College, the high school we started in Glen Forrest in 1988 as an extension of Helena School. Another ex-student of the Loco Shed school, Tony Taylor, who works for the trust as well, couldn't make the 2018 reunion, but his two older sisters, Cynthia and Jane, were both there.

After the reunion, Kevin took Tom and me out bush to revisit the *Bukli* meeting ground, the old dry riverbed, before taking us on to a block of land at Kedjerina that was run by the trust. There were a few houses and a large water tank, and he explained the trust's plans for it. The whole experience—going out bush, seeing them establish their own area—was wonderful.

I had arranged to meet Daisy Tinker a couple of days after the reunion, and this time she brought her son Phillip with her. Phillip had been the baby we had practised mothercraft on at the Loco Shed. It was so lovely to meet the man I had only known as a baby, who now wants me to be his grandma. I have a lovely photo of Phillip and me from that day.

Daisy has kidney problems and attends the Port Hedland hospital for dialysis, so, whenever I go to Port Hedland, I call in to the hospital to visit her, and I've sometimes seen some of my other students there. This was the last place I saw Tommy Gardner. I was told that he had been hit by a car and had suffered some sort of brain damage and could hardly talk. When I went to leave, he put his hand on his heart, looked at me and stammered, 'Skoodidja, skoodidja.' Just like he had done when he was a child, and when I was his skoodidja, his schoolteacher. I left him photos of the school days and old copies of the Mili Mili that contained some of his stories, so he could share them with his family.

It makes me feel so sad that so many of these lovely students I had are dying because of drink and drugs. Don McLeod had a point, keeping them in the bush for as long as he could.

62

REFLECTION

Covid19 is with us. I am, as usual, feeling very lucky. Because all the workshops and activities that I would normally have been doing have been cancelled, I have had time to think about, and write notes about, my history. But I also worry about those who are suffering at this time.

In our little village of Darlington, where Tom and I returned and bought the school, we have always had great neighbours, but during the height of the pandemic, we felt especially lucky. We have two lovely families living on two sides of us and a very friendly couple on the third. There are nine kids altogether in these three families and, because they were all home from school and the couple on one side had to work from home, there was more activity going on around us than there would have been if the lockdown hadn't happened.

The ANZAC dawn service in the dark on 25 April 2020 will be a time never to be forgotten. I joined a family who lives up the hill as the mum and son played the 'Last Post' and the 'Reveille' on trombone and French horn. Hand torches were on up and down the street and I heard that other groups around the village were doing the same thing. A neighbour from down the hill yelled out, 'Thank you.' I felt like hugging everybody, but of course we couldn't.

This time has been one of great reflection. I was lucky to have been born into a loving and conscientious family in 1935. Both parents had lived through a world war and a depression, before having children before and during a second world war. Dad had studied and worked his way into a good job; Mum was a very maternal and devoted wife. My four siblings and I still look back and appreciate what a fantastic childhood we had in Darlington with its creeks, hills, school and good friends. With plenty of space to play, with bike-riding and cubby-building. With chooks, a garden and a cow. Mum and Dad were great role models as parents and partners. All five of us have also had lasting happy marriages, and we take delight in our children and grandchildren.

I was blessed to have people I looked up to and gained valuable guidance from. Mollie Skinner, in her work with and for Aboriginal people; the wonderful Kath Skipsey, who taught me so many important values, especially how to try to smile and sing my way through any difficulties; my father, with his strength to do what he believed was right; my mother, who volunteered on many committees and who made do with whatever she had; and both of my parents with their search for peace through non-violence.

ACKNOWLEDGMENTS

FROM SALLY

Thank you very much to Freda for encouraging me and being so skilful as an author. She has been able to condense and enliven so many of my memories. My mother, Elsie Gare, saved all of the letters I wrote home—about one per week— from Oombulgurri and Port Hedland. Dad, Cyril Gare, saved copies of letters that he wrote and received when helping Aboriginal groups from the mid-forties onwards.

The people at Oombulgurri who included me in so many cultural and other activities, made me feel as though I was related to them. They even gave me a 'skin name'. This feeling is kept alive when I have contact with children and grandchildren of my ex-students, who converse with me on Facebook.

Thank you to Jack and Joyce Glass with whom I stayed in Port Hedland. They looked after me and were very supportive of what I was doing at the school and around the town.

Now, The Pindan Mob! They trusted me and included me in so many ceremonial activities as well as weekend fishing and hunting. A special thanks goes to Ernie Mitchell and Peter Coffin and their families for treating me like family too. Some of their relatives have also helped me with information for this great collection of memories.

In both Oombulgurri and Two Mile, I can definitely acknowledge the people as the traditional custodians of the land because they did look after it and treated it with care and respect.

Over the last nearly three years, apart from Freda, my main help has been from my husband Tom. He could use the appropriate technology for improving and sending photos, and really showed an interest in what I was doing. I appreciated his suggestions and couldn't help remembering how we met. Both Oombulgurri and Port Hedland were very important in the development of our relationship. We will be celebrating our sixtieth wedding anniversary just a couple of months before this book is published.

Thank you to Allen & Unwin for accepting my story. I hope to work with you on the next eventful sixty years.

FROM FREDA

Every student deserves a teacher like Sally. I was lucky enough to start my education at Helena School in 1970 where Sally undertook relief teaching the following year. It was a small private school descended from a much earlier era and, if I remember correctly, there were only about forty of us in total, with a handful of boarders from colonial Malaya or rural Western Australia. The two old ladies who owned the school terrified me and I was instantly drawn to Sally with her easy manner and obvious love of teaching.

While writing this book I recalled some of my earliest memories of that time with her, such as making a banner with every student printing a fallen deciduous leaf on it, the title AUTUMN across its top in big letters. It was placed on the wall of our single classroom with its little fireplace in the corner, and Sally asked us all to tell her what autumn meant to us—cooler weather, warmer clothes, trees changing colour, the Easter bunny. Everyone had something to add. I would stare at that banner in fascination—how that strange combination of letters created a word that could encapsulate so much—when I probably should have been concentrating on something else. I was only five or six years of age, but Sally had ignited my love of the written word.

I credit Sally for many personal traits that I still hold dear—compassion, equality, and inclusion. She taught us all of this and more alongside what was required by the traditional education curriculum. When Sally and her husband Tom subsequently bought Helena School, and throughout the years I attended, the enrolments steadily rose, and included disabled children, a rarity in those days. Helena School, and Helena College, now goes through from Kindergarten to Year 12 and has grown into two separate campuses. It is a credit to both Sally and Tom. I feel privileged to have had Sally, and Helena, in my life.

Fast forward many years, and I was contacted by Sally's eldest son, John, who informed me his son Robert would be studying radiography at a university 'over east', in fact only an hour from our farm. We organised to meet, and it felt like we were still in high school together. Easy conversations, much laughter, and a tale or two about Sally. Not the Sally

I remembered, but a younger teacher starting out in an incredible part of the world, outback Western Australia.

I thank Sally for trusting me with her story. I have loved every minute speaking with and listening to this remarkable woman. I only apologise with border closures and Covid that it has taken so long. Heartfelt thanks to her husband Tom for his expert computer skills, sharing large documents and photographs with me digitally. A big thank you, too, to all of her wonderful, caring family. We were extremely lucky that Sally's mother kept all of the letters from Sally while she lived in the Nor'West. They were invaluable in writing this story, and gave an insight into a young, inexperienced woman maturing and growing stronger in the outback.

I need to also thank the wonderful staff at Allen & Unwin, especially Rebecca Kaiser and Richard Walsh. You are amazing to work with and feel more like friends than colleagues. Thank you for bringing great stories to light.

Lastly, but far from least, my family—you are my world. Thank you for putting up with having a writer in the mix.